CRAZY LUCKY

REMARKABLE STORIES FROM
INSIDE THE WORLD OF **CELEBRITY ICONS**

JOHN MASON

FOREWORD BY **PRISCILLA PRESLEY**

un 🐦

LOS ANGELES, CA

To Cindy Pearlman, without whom I would never have finished this book, and my wonderful editor, John Cerullo.

To my family, past, present, and future, who I hope will treasure these stories, some of which they have even lived through.

And most important, to my friend and client of almost fifty years, Olivia Newton-John, who gave joy to the world and who never changed during her amazing career. I would not have mine without her.

CONTENTS

FOREWORD
By Priscilla Presley

B efore I became an actress, I opened a boutique clothing shop in Beverly Hills. It was called Bis & Beau. That was back in 1973, following my separation from Elvis. I had no real plans, only to find a path for myself. One day, a young man walked in and very politely introduced himself, complimenting me on my new venture. He was a little shy, and so was I. Our exchange was brief but pleasant.

A decade later, a friend recommended a lawyer to me. I learned this man was none other than John Mason. I might not have remembered our short exchange at my shop, but he did and reminded me. We have now been friends for something like forty years.

When I met John, he had already helped many people I knew deeply and admired, such as Frankie Valli, Donna Summer, Olivia Newton-John, Kenny Rogers, and even Quincy Jones. For me, he helped navigate negotiations with Elvis Presley Enterprises, the London Symphony Orchestra, and RCA Records. I was struck by his kindness and loyalty, as well as his deep commitment to representing my interests. I even introduced him to my daughter, Lisa Marie, whom he took care of as well.

Artist management has always seemed to focus on making commissions, rather than prioritizing what is best for the artist.

Having John in my corner helped me realize that. I think if Elvis had a John Mason in his corner, things might have turned out very differently for him.

Over the years, John and I have become dear friends. His wife, Bianca, as well. We have spent some special times together and have often looked back at the incredible personalities and tremendous talent we have been fortunate to work with. There have been good times and certainly hard ones as well. John has always been there to support me and his legendary clients.

In *Crazy Lucky*, John's own story weaves in and out of the lives of some of the entertainment world's most extraordinary talents. You will find a common theme: His ability to see the person behind the star.

INTRODUCTION

I don't come from show business.

We didn't even have a TV until I was six years old. And when we got one, there wasn't much to see on that tiny black-and-white screen. I idolized the cowboy stars but didn't think I would ever meet one. My dad was a butcher, and my mom, a grocery checker. I had no thoughts of being an actor or even going to auditions (like so many kids in LA at the time), so I was truly shocked, in 1955, when Karen Pendleton, the girl sitting next to me at Fair Avenue Elementary, was plucked from our midst to be a Mouseketeer by Walt Disney himself. She never came back to class because of her new work schedule. For a nine-year-old, this seemed too crazy. Walt even hired teachers to be on the set with all those kids.

Sounded like heaven, but wasn't Hollywood all about the illusion? Turns out, it was a tough life and Karen's career, like many other child actors, was short lived. Still, I thought, *Wow! Karen is a star and must be loving her life.*

How could I know until the proverbial curtain was ripped back?

Just a few years later, my classmate and friend Paul Petersen was plucked from our school to play Donna's son on *The Donna Reid Show*, which ran from 1958 through 1966. He also got to star with the incredible Sally Field on an episode of *The Flying*

Nun. I thought he was the coolest guy I ever knew because he was on TV and, later, the big screen. However, in real life, Paul told people he felt exploited, and he ultimately became an advocate for better working conditions for child actors. He founded the organization A Minor Consideration to help former child actors make the transition from screen life to real life.

My friends' successes and celebrity resonated with me. I still didn't have the acting bug, but I did dream of being a singing cowboy. To that end, I learned how to ride a horse and play the guitar at the same time. The big problem was I couldn't sing! A small pivot, and I ditched the horse but kept the guitar. I worked hard enough and became good enough to play in some successful bands and was even hired to do a few shows with lots of other great bands and singers, including playing in Frankie Avalon's band in the 1965 movie *I'll Take Sweden*.

Frankie was wonderful to me and remains a friend and client nearly sixty years later.

I wish I could say that every big star was that wonderful.

Bob Hope, one of the biggest stars in the world back in the day, also came into my orbit on the set of *I'll Take Sweden*. I thought he would be the same nice and funny man in person, so I walked up to him at a rehearsal at Paramount Pictures one day and introduced myself. Bob Hope didn't care. I will never forget his response:

"Go away, kid. You're bothering me."

I didn't need to be told twice.

✦

But the grind of a music career, or potential acting career, was already wearing on me. I experienced the demanding work schedule and the pressure to always top your last performance, while also coping with the nonstop travel, the long hours, and the days away from home.

On the other hand, I had noticed something: I loved the business of show business. I was the band member who dealt with the union demands as a member of the Local 47 of the American Federation of Musicians. I was the one who reviewed and signed our contracts. I even filed a labor relations claim against a big music star who'd stiffed my band on money from a tour. We won, and the celeb was not allowed to hire any musicians for his shows or recording purposes until we were paid in full. I did the paperwork and consider that my first settlement.

That was it. I found my calling.

I would become a lawyer for celebrities, but I had a big question: How do you do that?

The answer: You start at the bottom, including four years of college, then three years of law school. What I hadn't thought of until I finished those seven years was that I might not be hired by anyone—clients or law firms. Much like all law students, even today, I started applying early for jobs, focusing on law firms with celebrity clients, television networks, movie studios, and record companies. It wasn't long before I was a practicing lawyer in Beverly Hills getting Jack Lemmon's mother out of a legal jam. Jack was so grateful that he took this kid to lunch, but more on that in another chapter.

The jobs got better, the stars got bigger, and the world of show business was beyond my wildest dreams.

I got lucky.

Crazy lucky.

◆

This is the story of how a kid whose parents worked in a grocery store became the attorney and confidant of some of the most high-profile celebrities the world has ever known. These pages include the true never-before-told accounts of how I met and was invited into the inner circles of Gloria Estefan, Michael Jackson, Shakira, Olivia Newton-John, and so many more stars who orbited my life. My decades-long experiences with my clients were both personal and business. And what happened behind the curtains, backstage, inside their mansions, and on their private planes on trips across the world was more than crazy. It was magic.

The marriages and the divorces, the children and the exes, the affairs, accidents, deaths, illnesses, triumphs, and comebacks, and the managers, agents, and deals, deals, deals. I was part of it all. Ultimately, it was my job when a star would call at three in the morning with the kind of problem you don't want to read in the headlines or gossip columns.

"John, just deal with it," I would hear.

And I did—and still do.

Their stories are weaved into my own life story, which will also unfold in the pages before you. I hope you enjoy reading these true behind-the-scenes tales as much as I enjoyed remembering and writing about them. Above all, I hope you'll also feel a deeper bond with some of your favorites celebrities as you get to know the real person. You might even shed a tear of sympathy for the toll fame took on their lives.

Many of the bold faces in this book paid the ultimate price for their dream.

Were they crazy lucky, or were they sometimes just crazy?

CRAZY LUCKY

1

THE BUTCHER'S SON

*"I was officially making a living
in the entertainment business."*

There is almost nothing about my story that serves as a "coming attraction" to a life in entertainment law. A sea captain or a butcher, maybe. A lawyer? No way!

My story is, however, an adventure most lawyers, including me, don't ever dream of. It's the kind of stuff that makes a good "based on a true story" movie. It dates back to the early 1700s in Scotland, where the Mason men were sea captains and the Mason women managed households, hoping that the men survived capsizing boats, hurricane-like storms, and your occasional shark or whale attack.

My grandfather David Mason was born in 1881. What a character he was, with his northern English accent, a big, bushy mustache (frequently used to tickle me when we hugged), and a hilarious sense of humor. To this day, people say, "How could your father's father have been born in 1881 and still be a part of your life?" Well, the math is pretty simple. He lived to be eighty-two, so from 1946 until after my sixteenth birthday, he was a huge part of my life. Grandpa David was the first crazy lucky guy in our family and the first who decided he was going to be in show business. He was actually cast in quite a few movies but wasn't fated to have a huge career in front of the camera. He wound up a security guard at the famous Paramount Pictures front gate.

His early life would have made a good movie. At the age of thirteen, my grandfather signed a five-year contract to work as an indentured seaman, a backbreaking job filled with risk of injuries and illnesses and one that sustained a greater casualty rate than almost any other job on the sea. These seafaring workers could not quit until their contract ran out, if they survived that long. Running away while in port was not a great option, as you could be arrested, jailed, or killed in the process. He hated being on the ship, and in 1895, he broke his contract at the ship's first stop in Nova Scotia and went west, escaping to the wilds of Alberta, Canada, where he joined the Royal Canadian Mounted Police (the Mounties). It was in Alberta where he met and married a lovely lady named Lily Hobson, who was given fine silverware to celebrate their marriage. The same knives, forks, and spoons can be found on my dining room table today.

Eventually, my grandparents came to Los Angeles so he could fulfill his dream of acting in the fledgling movie business. There is a framed photo I treasure of him straddling a big brown quarter horse with an old-style movie camera behind him on the set of a movie whose title remains a mystery. You have to give it to my grandfather's persistence in life. He went from a servant on a ship, to a fugitive, to a member of the Canadian Mounties, to an actor in glamorous early Hollywood. Nothing makes me smile like that dusty, browned picture of him. And he passed on the trait of refusing to take no for an answer.

My father was an American baby, a Mason who was born in Venice, California. His early life was tragic because, soon after his arrival, his mother died. She left behind a husband who was determined to be a star and worked steadily now as a movie stuntman. He didn't have the bandwidth or the know-how to deal with a six-month-old baby, so my dad was shipped to his grandparents to be raised in Canada. My dad went to school in Penticton, British Columbia, where he learned the trade of butchering from his mother's parents. They trained him to work in their shop, but the lure of Hollywood and a desire to rejoin his dad was just too strong. He packed up and left before even going to high school; no formal education was required for his trade. Back in Los Angeles at the start of the United States' military involvement in World War II, as an American citizen he was drafted by the army and sent to El Paso, Texas, for basic training. Soon after, he was shipped off to Italy for three years. He came back older and wiser in 1945.

✦

A quick note about my mother, whose maiden name was Vallee. My mother's great-grandfather and the rest of the family emigrated from France in the late 1700s to Canada. The Masons and Vallees never met because one family was in eastern Canada and the other in western Canada. Eventually, my great-great-grandfather Vallee immigrated to Wisconsin in the United States.

My mother's grandfather became quite active in the Civil War, which one day would inspire my wife, Bianca, and me to visit Racine, Wisconsin, where he raised his artillery battery and is buried. He served four years as a captain in the Union army. (During our visit to Racine, we brought his ancient sword to his grave and later to his hometown, Beloit, where we shared them with the community by taking them to the Beloit Historical

Center, where they were on exhibit. The hilt of the sword read "Presented to Captain John F. Valee by his Co. 4th Battery Wis. Artillery.") Eventually, he settled with his wife in Madison, where my mother's father, John Vallee, was born.

Unlike the Mason clan of only one child per generation, my mother was one of five sisters. One of the girls had breathing problems, and doctors at the time insisted that a move to a more temperate climate could help, which turned out to be Los Angeles. Sadly, while driving across the country to their new home, the ill sister died. The rest decided to keep pushing on with the dream to live out west in California. My mother was born in Los Angeles.

All of this brings the story to me—almost. A cousin introduced my parents. They fell in love and were married before my dad was shipped out to El Paso for basic training. In the army, he was a cook, thanks to his skills as a butcher. Four years later, he returned to LA and got a job as a butcher at a local market. My mom also got a job there as a checker.

Just like in the movie *The Best Years of Our Lives*, they spent the postwar years settling down. It wasn't long before I was born. Dad bought a cracker box house in North Hollywood for $20,000 thanks to the GI Bill. There was no air-conditioning or central heating. If you closed your bedroom door, you got no heat. Funny, but I took my grown son to that little house five years ago, so he could get a feeling about my childhood. It's still a small cracker box house owned by others now. We stood outside of it, and I said, "Sam, I'm going to show you the inside of the house if the people allow it." A quick knock on the door, and we received a friendly "Come on in." I was able to take Sam through all the rooms, which was really fun. My childhood bedroom was exactly the same but felt smaller, as these things usually do.

Houses don't shrink. Our perspective just widens.

By all accounts, it was a wonderful childhood. Inspired by my grandfather and his horse stunts, my dad made sure that his only son started riding horses five days a week at age five. The rest of my time was spent at school and hanging out with neighborhood kids. We didn't have a television, so I'd log time at the neighbors' watching Gene Autry and Roy Rogers ride, rope, sing, and do good deeds. They were my first star icons—in the days before I worked with celebrity icons.

One day, I made a career decision. I went into my parents' bedroom and announced that I was going to be a singing cowboy. It was the mid-'50s, and there were many other little boys making that same pronouncement to their doubtful parents. It seemed plausible to me, but there was a problem with the singing cowboy thing. I couldn't sing.

Not that I would let this fact deter me from a career in the music business. I transitioned from singing on a four-legged creature to playing guitar. The year was 1956, and Elvis was killing it with "Heartbreak Hotel" and "Don't Be Cruel." I was nine and musically impressionable, and I got my first guitar for my tenth birthday.

This wasn't the usual strum in your room until your parents want to break the guitar over your head. By August 1957, I was able to read sheet music. Friends asked me to play, and I learned all the songs on the charts. I was ready for the next step, because one thing was certain: To borrow some '60s lingo, dig it, I could really play the guitar. I was the coolest. And it actually sounded like what I heard on the radio.

My new craft is why I walked right into the local Sears, Roebuck & Company in North Hollywood to look at guitars one summer day. Sears's in-store brand was Silvertone, and it sold lots of music books as well.

"Do you play, kid?" asked a salesman.

He handed me a guitar right off the rack, and man, did I show him.

And just like that . . . Sears offered me a job.

"We would like to hire you to sit in here and play guitar for the customers. You'll use our books of sheet music. People will buy both the guitars and the sheet music," he said.

In 1958, I couldn't drive, enlist in the army, or get a girl to go on a date with me.

However, I was officially making a living in the entertainment business.

In some ways, it's not a joke. By age thirteen, even though I was still taking weekly guitar lessons, I was working at Sears on weekday evenings (on Saturdays, I worked in the meat market). I had to take the bus, and on my way from North Hollywood to downtown Los Angeles, I would pass the musicians union, Local 47. One day, I decided to join the union so I could gig with my fellow musicians and got off the bus at the Local 47 stop and popped into the union office.

"You can apply," said the nice lady behind the desk who seemed to be laughing at this kid who had no business joining any organization outside of maybe the Boy Scouts.

Determined, I filled out the form and checked the boxes indicating that I could read sheet music and play with the best of them.

A week later, a letter arrived at the Mason house. "Congratulations on your acceptance into the Musicians Union, Local 47," it read. I'm happy to give them a shout-out now, appreciating the fact that they did not dabble in age discrimination. My information was on file with them now, and it wasn't long before musical groups in need of a guitarist were calling because they needed someone who could actually sight-read music.

It was 1961 by now. Dion was rocking out with "Runaround Sue," Ricky Nelson had a hit with "Travelin' Man," and the Shirelles were "Dedicated to the One I Love." They were doing well in show business.

And so was I.

High school wasn't a challenge for me. I was a solid student who could work gigs at night and do high school in my sleep. Fortunately, a guy named Mike Todd called when I was only in the tenth grade. He asked if I'd like to be his band's guitarist. The group was called the Marketts, and the lineup featured Michael Z. Gordon and various session musicians from the LA area, including the great drummer Hal Blaine. We had that surf rock sound, which was made popular by the Beach Boys, and our own hit called "Surfer's Stomp."

Our biggest hit was a tune called "Out of Limits," originally called "Outer Limits" and named after the 1963 TV series. A quick legal fact: Leslie Stevens, creator of *The Outer Limits*, sued the Marketts for using the words from his TV series. That resulted in the title change. It wasn't long before I was in school by day and in the studio at night. I also got to play lots of gigs.

Vocal groups ruled the charts, and virtually none of them had backup bands. So, the "instrumental" hitmakers had to back up the singers, even the soloists. If you didn't see "& the . . ." after an artist's name, they didn't have a band. Unfortunately, we never got rehearsal time with singers until just before the shows, always in a small room with bad acoustics and no charts. When we knew whom we would be backing up, we would buy their records so we could try to learn the chords, solos, and parts. That didn't always work out. I will never forget the night we were backing up the Castells on their great hit "Sacred." When the beautiful and complicated guitar solo came up, I froze. Three good notes followed by thirty seconds of garbage. A deeply humbling experience.

Another "humbling" happened in a rehearsal room at Sun Valley Junior High School, where we were backing up Caesar and Cleo, soon to be known as Sonny and Cher. I couldn't play because I couldn't take my eyes off the gorgeous dark-haired, dark-eyed young Cherilyn Sarkisian. Sonny Bono leaned forward and said, "Don't even think about it." Little did I know that they were engaged as well as being singing partners.

It never changes: Join a band and everyone loves you. I was becoming pretty popular at my high school, because on the weekends, I was on TV being featured in all those *American Bandstand* type of shows. By age sixteen, I had enough money saved up to buy my own grown-up Chevy Impala convertible, and my friends would unzip the back window and climb in. I'd come out of the studio or a class at school, and people would already be in my car waiting to go cruising with me.

It was the summer of 1964, and all you needed on a hot summer night in LA was a cool car to cruise Sunset Boulevard. I was gigging with groups including the Routers by now and earning really good money. I even played a few shows with the Beach Boys. I knew Carl Wilson through high school friends and the music circuit. I ran into the group a lot and found them super cool and enormously talented.

Early signs of my future legal career emerged that same year, too. Musicians notoriously have trouble getting paid, and I insisted that some of the groups I played with go to the musicians union to fix a few dicey situations where our youth meant we were getting the short end of the stick. We won our "cases," which felt quite satisfying. Wheels began to turn in my head. Maybe if a career in music didn't work out, I'd explore going behind the scenes.

My senior year in high school, I met a girl who was going off to college at UCLA. The truth was I had never really thought about college, and my parents didn't push it. They were trade people, and college just wasn't on their radar. Meanwhile, I thought, *Maybe I should apply to UCLA*. I filled out the paperwork, and soon a big acceptance packet arrived in the mail.

The following August, I took my first steps onto an actual college campus. A few weeks into school, and I found out that gigging at night and touring didn't mesh well coursework. College was a lot more challenging than high school, which meant I had to quit all the touring bands to focus on my studies. I started teaching for a mobile guitar lesson school. I'd drive all over LA to teach kids. I was still living at home with my parents despite the "fortune" I was making giving guitar lessons to eight-year-olds.

The lure of music was too strong. Eventually, I formed another band, the Continentals, and we were booked solid for frat parties at UCLA and USC, among other collegiate events, and also for weddings, bar mitzvahs, and various gigs throughout Southern California.

I was making more money than my dad did on an annual basis by performing with bands. The great part of this was my parents never had to pay a dime for college or law school.

Yes, law school.

A little bit of soul-searching later, and I wasn't sure that becoming a musician was my end game, although I still enjoyed performing. The idea of law school had been floating around my brain, but there were no lawyers in the family to give me any advice. I heard from friends, "You should go to the East Coast for law school." I had never been out east.

I applied to Harvard, Yale, Stanford, and the University of California, Berkeley. I wasn't sure how I was going to pay for any of them, but it was time to narrow the list down, even though I didn't think I could handle the winters in the east. When the acceptance letter arrived from Berkeley, I glanced at the $3,000-a-year price tag and shook my head. But when it offered me a full scholarship, the idea of going to law school there became a no-brainer.

In September 1968, I left home to study with some of the smartest students around on Berkeley's incredible campus (and it still is—the college is gorgeous). I didn't realize at first that everyone who goes to these types of schools is the top of the top. Quickly, I found out that law school would be a supercompetitive situation. At UCLA, I did do well, but now it was at a higher pitch. We had a five-point grading scale, and the push was to graduate at the top of your class, which would then guarantee you a job. I welcomed any help, because the truth was I had never met a real lawyer.

The summer after my first year in law school, I decided to stop performing to focus on getting ready for school, which meant my income was a big zero. Overall, it was a positive time, because I had my scholarship and savings. I lost thirty pounds and didn't stress out performing. It was odd not to have a job, but I tried to enjoy my last years in school.

I was pretty naive back in 1968. I loved the Cal campus and the law school building, the dean, students, and professors. We were

at the top right-hand corner of the campus, so we were not physically or mentally close to the undergraduates. However, I became
aware of the free speech movement and the protesters' demand
that students should basically run the university, saying and doing
whatever they wanted. This was also the era of hippies and free
love in San Francisco. It all seemed innocuous . . . . until it wasn't.

A relatively unexceptional event turned into days of rioting
back in May 1969, the end of my first year in law school and the
week before finals. Each day, I walked to the law school from my
Berkeley apartment on College Avenue. It was a beautiful campus
with large concrete buildings offset by greenery, seasonal flowers,
and towering trees. I passed a two-block lot that students and local
residents were allowed to use for private vegetable gardens. For
many reasons, almost irrelevant today, the university announced
that it was going to tear down the park and redevelop the area. At
about 4:30 in the morning on May 15, 1969, hundreds of California Highway Patrol and Berkeley police officers cleared and fenced
People's Park.

Student unrest was at its zenith, and by noon, thousands of
protesters (not all were students) appeared in the main plaza of
the campus. I wandered over and heard the booming voice of our
student body president, who was speaking through a professional
sound system.

"Let's take the park!" he shouted into the mic.

"We want the park! We want the park!" screamed the protesters
as they raced off campus like an anthill emptying at a picnic. A
true riot had developed, and the California National Guard was
called in to "occupy" the campus and surrounding areas. For two
months, soldiers patrolled there and were more aggressive than I
could have ever imagined.

One foggy day, I was walking and stopped cold when a guardsman actually pointed his rifle, with bayonet in place, inches from my chest from less than a foot away. Maybe my big red beard made me look like a protester. I was not.

"Where do you think you're going?" he demanded, finger on the trigger.

"To the bookstore," I replied calmly. "It's right behind you. I am a law student, and you are making our lives miserable."

He lowered his rifle and let me go. Yet, I will never forget that incident, which will always color my experience with "authority."

The occupation finally ended, and by the time I returned for my senior year in August, the campus was back to normal. As graduation neared on May 15, 1971, I had already worked as a managing editor of the *California Law Review* and helped found *Ecology Law Quarterly*. It was an unforgettable time, but I was ready for the real world.

First things first: Graduation was in a lovely courtyard on the side of the main law building. Our class decided not to have a traditional speaker, such as a judge, deliver the commencement speech at our graduation and elected me to reach out and sign two-time Academy Award winner Peter Ustinov. It was the first test of my entertainment lawyer "career." I would negotiate with Hollywood royalty.

And so I did. After tracking down Ustinov's agent and making my pitch, the reply surprised me: "Mr. Ustinov would be honored to speak at your graduation. He will not charge a fee and will make his own way up there."

We got him a black robe, and he was brilliant, charming, and witty. Ustinov was a major star and the first one I met. His bushy beard and English accent reminded me of my grandfather.

Known back then as a raconteur, his off-color stories of his life and those of his costars were hilarious, though he clearly knew nothing of the law. I wonder if he even had a lawyer.

Other areas of life weren't as great. My parents had gotten divorced, which was their solution to the fact that my dad drank too much and Mom had an affair. In fact, my mom called two weeks before graduation to tell me she would be getting married to her boyfriend during her trip up to celebrate and that I needed to provide the judge. Suddenly, my actual graduation became as much about planning her wedding as collecting my diploma. In the end, I found a judge, and they said their vows that morning right in front of where Mr. Ustinov would later make his speech.

The ink was barely dry on my diploma, but I had a plan. I knew I wanted to be an entertainment lawyer, but I had never come close to that species. The only thing to do postgraduation was to get out there and apply for jobs.

One position opened up with an emphasis on entertainment litigation, in where else but Beverly Hills.

2

EARLY DAYS:
A YOUNG LAWYER IN HOLLYWOOD

B y your third year of law school, it's time to start thinking about the so-called real world and begin the process of applying for jobs. I was a butcher's son without any connections, but I was also third in my class at UC Berkeley School of Law. I sent out my résumé and had a bunch of interviews with entertainment firms in Los Angeles. A few turned me down. One offered to meet me, but there was no offer of employment. I saw their memo about me in a file years later, which said, "We didn't like his tie!"

As disappointed as I was, I still needed a job and pressed on. My ego and patience kept me going. I still had a cool car from my guitar star days, a red 1968 Corvette Stingray with the big 427 V-8 engine. It really stood out in the parking lot of North Hollywood's Chateau Whitsett Apartments, where I studied for the bar by the pool every day, back in 1971. A starting salary in law when I passed the bar was $15,000 per year. My friend and next-door neighbor at the time was a pharmacist earning close to $60,000. The thought that I might have chosen the wrong profession crossed my mind daily.

In the meantime, I thought that maybe if I had my own clients, I could get a job. I remembered that back in Berkeley, I read a story in the *San Francisco Chronicle* about my friend and former bandmate Mike Curb, who had sold his music production company to MGM and was made president of MGM Records. I called his office to ask if he had any outside legal work I could take on. The receptionist said, "Mr. Curb is no longer with the company." What the hell? I called him at home, and he told me he had been pushed out over a stock dispute.

By May 1971, my path would lead me to a solid first job with a law firm in Beverly Hills. Remember, these were the days before the internet, so there was no website to look it up. I went in for an interview; they said they were in the entertainment business, which wasn't exactly true. Instead, the firm was a tax and real estate planning group with a few clients in showbiz. Real life law work begins . . . at the bottom.

The people were nice enough, but I hated it. Doing estate planning is just as "dead" as it sounds. You sit there with clients who are depressed thinking about where their assets will go after they die, and maybe you get a thousand-dollar fee. When the client does "move on," you're the lawyer for the estate, but only partners in the firm got to do that work.

I kept trying to get into a bigger firm with a solid entertainment practice, and finally my phone rang in February 1972. "We have a position in entertainment litigation," said the voice on the other end of the line. "We can move you over to entertainment someday." The firm, Kaplan, Livingston, Goodwin, Berkowitz & Selvin, was perfect because it had been in movies and television for more than thirty years. Its reputation was excellent and its clients famous, primarily actors, directors, writers, and producers.

I had interviewed with this firm back in my third year at Berkeley. However, it didn't invite me down to its offices at 450

North Roxbury in Beverly Hills for another year. The firm occupied the top three floors, and my office looked down on "Little" Santa Monica Boulevard and the Flats of Beverly Hills. In those days, offices were much larger than they are now, so I was able to furnish mine with a cool antique desk that I still write on today.

I was at the bottom of the lawyer pool on my first litigation case, but at least it was for a notable star. Upper management put me on *Cary Grant v. Universal Pictures*, with us on Cary's side. This was incredible because I loved Cary Grant movies as a kid. All of a sudden, I was helping one of the biggest movie stars on the planet fight one of the biggest studios, which was not only enjoyable but actually quite technical. The question was: How do you define gross versus net profits in the movie business? It's still a huge issue that gets litigated all the time, although Cary had the balls to ask the question when it was an unspoken rule to never go against the studios.

Needless to say, I learned all the tricks the studios play from my early cases and would use this information and knowledge against them countless times in my career. It all started with Cary, but later I would learn that nothing ever changes in Hollywood. The studios still screw around with everyone. They've been at it since the first flicker on a silver screen.

You have to remember that in the golden years of moviemaking, few talents would actually sue, but then came TV, which was a new medium in several ways. By the 1970s, stars began to speak out in dribs and drabs, not in droves. The brave ones wanted their fair share of the money and didn't believe in bad deals or creative accounting.

The studio system in those days meant that actors signed long-term contracts when they were "nobodies." Most signed at a cheap rate because it was better than having no contract, which was a huge mistake because most actors didn't know how it "worked" in those days. And then if they hit stardom, they were basically duped out of the profits of most of their films or TV shows.

My goal from day one was to prevent my clients from signing those terrible deals and to renegotiate if they had done so before meeting me. In one way, the movie studios (not TV or music companies) made it easier by generally not requiring contracts to be negotiated by lawyers. They would stick some paper in the hands of an actor and say, "Sign it." As I learned in Cary Grant's case, the studios would spend big bucks on certain movies (the surefire hits) and then dump the loser films in with the winners to recover all of it. (This type of "accounting" is nearly impossible now because each film is treated separately and there are just so many ways to exploit each one. I used "nearly" because they still try. Scarlett Johansson sued Disney for releasing her 2021 film *Black Widow* through a license to its Disney+ streaming channel rather than in theaters, where her profit participation would have come from ticket sales.)

The old days had the old ways. Take Cary Grant's 1964 film, *Father Goose*, a Technicolor rom-com set during World War II, which also starred Leslie Caron and Trevor Howard. Some called it the penultimate film of Grant's long career, and it even won an Oscar for original screenplay. Grant was a maverick, as was John Wayne. These were stars who wanted to break out and earn what they were owed. The film was a hit, and Grant wanted his fair share, which is why he hired our firm. He wasn't really concerned about "not working again." He had worked most of his life and was an icon. Being at the bottom of the totem pole, I never met Mr. Grant, but my work on that case led to more responsibility.

In Grant's case, Universal Pictures settled, which was a huge victory for the firm and Cary Grant. I got bumped up to handling some legal affairs for Katharine Hepburn, Jack Lemmon, and the director Sidney Lumet, who called the shots for *12 Angry Men*, plus the Al Pacino classics *Dog Day Afternoon* and *Serpico*. I was still at the bottom, but not rock bottom.

The firm I worked for respected artists trying to get their fair share while also maintaining their lives, which meant the work included wills, divorces, etc. The job required me to handle whatever came up legally for them. I'll never forget the day when one of the partners at the firm called me into his office with an emergency that needed to be kept out of the press.

"John, I was just told that Jack Lemmon's mother-in-law was arrested for reckless driving, and I need you to handle the case. Jack wants us to take care of it. *Now.*"

It turns out that she lived with Jack, his wife, and their young children. The mother-in-law's job was to take care of the kids, including driving the little ones to school. She must have been running late that day, because she blew through a stop sign in Beverly Hills. An officer saw the whole thing and pulled her over. The cops threw the book at her, with charges of speeding and reckless endangerment. In her defense, it was just one stop sign. The minus: She could have T-boned someone else's family.

I couldn't tell the Lemmon family that I wasn't really familiar with these kinds of cases. But I knew that somehow I would figure it out to my client's advantage. In court, I went right up to the prosecutor's table before the judge arrived and said, "Here's the story. Jack Lemmon's mother-in-law ran a stop sign taking his children to school. I've never been to court. What should I do?"

"Here's what I can do," said the prosecutor with a smile. "She pleads guilty to missing the stop sign, and we fine her one hundred dollars. She doesn't have to do anything else."

"I'll call Mr. Lemmon," I replied.

A senior partner actually called Mr. Lemmon and then told me, "Absolutely, it's okay, but she's not going to pay the fine."

The judge let her off without paying. Jack was so thankful that he called me and invited me to lunch, where we talked about his long career and life in show business. Needless to say, being seen at a restaurant in Beverly Hills with an Oscar-winning movie star was great for my ego and career. Lemmon was just as wonderful as the characters he played. He must have enjoyed the lunch, too, because he even invited me to the set of a new movie he was making with Walter Matthau. In the end, I wasn't able to go because I was working on contracts for the screen legend Katharine Hepburn.

✦

The music business called to me more than TV or film—I wanted to pick up where I'd left off as a kid. Fortunately, one of the senior partners in our entertainment group did some work for music artists and knew of my interest in that area. He asked me to help with the hugely successful band Creedence Clearwater Revival (CCR). Sadly, for their fans, Tom Fogerty quit the band in 1971 citing animosity with his brother John, who had also angered founders Stu Cook and Doug "Cosmo" Clifford by refusing to write and sing on an entire album.

We were asked by Cook and Clifford to help with the dissolution of the band and an audit of their royalties at Fantasy Records, based, of all places, in Berkeley. John Fogerty wanted nothing to do with Fantasy, Cook, Clifford, or our firm. But, hey, I got into the music business.

I was the first young lawyer at the Kaplan firm to be interested in the music business, and back then, it was much smaller than film and television, so any partner with any connection to it referred the matter to me. In fact, the head of our tax group was consulted by the manager of superstar Cat Stevens for help in planning his US tour. Yusuf (as he is now known) had already experienced worldwide success with his albums *Tea for the Tiller-man* and *Teaser and the Firecat*. His manager, Barry Krost, and I immediately bonded, as I did with Yusuf, and we made some unprecedented deals for Yusuf with A&M Records for North America and Island Records for the rest of the world, including unheard-of record contracts with ownership of his recordings and songs.

Barry also connected me to another legend in the music industry. I will never forget working one day with Chris Blackwell, the owner of Island Records (who had discovered Bob Marley as well as Cat Stevens), while he was piloting his speedboat off the coast of Jamaica. The engine noise was deafening. We didn't have AirPods or noise-canceling headphones back in those days. He was the first person I knew who had a mobile phone, the huge kind that was basically military grade. It was thirteen inches tall, thick, and heavy as a brick. As I sat in my office, I could picture him, phone in one hand, steering the speedboat with the other. I was awestruck to be talking to a legend and amazed that, unlike other entertainment industry executives, he actually cared about what was fair for artists, alongside recognizing their genius.

Barry was charming and brilliant. I learned some great tactics from Barry, who had been a child actor in London. One time, we were at A&M Records negotiating for Yusuf when Barry slammed his fist on owner Jerry Moss's desk. His watch broke into pieces, flying all over the room. After the meeting, I said how sorry I was that he'd lost his watch. He laughed out loud and responded, "Darling, that was just a show. I bought that cheap watch just for the right moment to smash it in front of Jerry." Barry also had a theory that if you made yourself really exclusive and did a great job, then the people will come to you. He was right.

The business was and is all about good word of mouth and showing up in the right places. When I started, I had an unlisted phone number and didn't advertise. But I was in the right places. Barry had taken me many times to Ma Maison in West Hollywood where Wolfgang Puck was the chef and Patrick Terrail was the ringmaster. There was no available phone number, no way to make a reservation, and no prices on the menu. Mysteriously, Barry could get in at any time. So could Jack Nicholson, Ringo Starr, Elton John, and Marlon Brando, among most of the Hollywood and international elite. Thankfully, Barry always paid the bill.

What I took away and integrated into my practice when I started my own law firm in 1978 was to be exclusive, expensive, and the best anyone had ever been in representing talent. I would even have business cards printed with the knight chess piece used by Richard Boone's character in the western series *Have Gun— Will Travel*. I would go anywhere and up against anyone, especially the studios, networks, and music companies. I worked twenty-hour days and virtually every weekend to be available, independent, and expert. It worked for me and my clients.

But let's not jump too far ahead. Young lawyers in those days barely met the clients. It was always the agents and managers who dealt with the lawyers. Yusuf did come in with Barry quite a few times, but never alone. However, it was different when I visited Olivia Newton-John, whose career was exploding in 1973; everyone on Earth was infatuated with her. She had a manager who didn't have control over the legal side of her business. She told him she needed to meet people who worked for her. We first met during a break on her world tour. Olivia had just played Japan and had returned to the United States to play the Metropolitan Opera House in New York City. But more on that later.

Rewind back to my days as a lawyer in the entertainment group at Kaplan. I was assigned work with Harold Berkowitz, a senior partner who was the lead attorney for Tandem Productions, a film and television production company founded in 1958 by the director Bud Yorkin and the writer-producer Norman Lear. It had become the hottest company in Hollywood, producing such classic series as *All in the Family*, *Maude*, *Good Times*, *Diff'rent Strokes*, *Archie Bunker's Place*, and *Sanford and Son*, among a slew of other hit shows that also reflected the times.

I was put on the Tandem team at the bottom, as I moved from film to TV and before I hit my stride in music. It required eighty-hour weeks at the office, where I worked on all the agreements with the owners of the shows and the talent. It was a tough job with various twists and turns. With five top-rated shows on the air, almost all sold to the networks from pilots, I was drafting from scratch dozens of contracts for writers, directors, and actors, each with his or her own agent, manager, lawyer, publicist, and baggage. Coming from film, I didn't have enough forms, so I had to make up documents. For example, for the creation and ownership of art by Jimmie "JJ" Walker on *Good Times*, there was a contract.

I learned way back when that dealing with talent is an art and skill—and I was good in both departments. Take the case of the beloved actor Redd Foxx, who was a huge star on the successful series *Sanford and Son*. He was demanding to renegotiate his contract, to the point that he locked himself in his trailer while shooting an episode. I got the call to go to the set to figure something out that involved him working that day and not wasting tens of thousands of dollars of set time.

"Go over there and see if you can talk to him, John," said the senior lawyer.

My first thought: *I can't believe some of this shit. Correction: most of this shit.*

Knock-knock on the trailer door.

"Mr. Foxx, I am a lawyer for Tandem," I told him through the locked steel entryway. "We're giving you a new deal."

The door cracked open a tiny bit.

"Do you think you can get back to work?" I asked.

Foxx, it turns out, just needed some reassurances that he would be paid what he believed was fair. I promised and reassured him, and the trailer door opened. He was in the faux junkyard set within the next five minutes. Problem solved.

✦

Contract negotiations were just part of it. Despite all the work young lawyers do, the key to respect and more money is bringing in business. That turned out to be harder than I thought. How do you get clients when you are only twenty-five years old with little experience and no contacts?

Well, I had one! Even though Mike Curb had already been pushed out at MGM Records when I called searching for a job after graduation, a lawyer who was still left from Mike's reign must have felt sorry for me and ultimately hired me as a consultant on a part-time basis for $500 a month. MGM Records was soon sold to the Germany company PolyGram, which had great success around the world but not in the United States. As soon as PolyGram took over, my primary job was to get it out of contracts with artists Mike had signed. Surprisingly, one of the first artists to go was Sammy Davis Jr., even after his wonderful hit "The Candy Man," produced by Mike Curb and featuring the Mike Curb Congregation, a group he'd founded and recorded as. There were no other regular members. By the way, it was Sammy's only number one record.

I guess PolyGram didn't want its biggest hit artist to be a Mike Curb contract. For sure, its execs thought they had the "secret sauce" and brought in a revolving door of presidents who had successfully run their companies in foreign countries. Not one succeeded or lasted for more than six months.

One of the things I learned while working in a company is that if you keep your door closed, people don't see you. You won't ever get fired because you're not in the way. So, I kept my door closed when I was in the office doing contract work.

A new president named Jimmy Bowen changed that philosophy.

I heard that Jimmy, who had produced huge hits for Frank Sinatra, Dean Martin, and even Sammy, was going to come by the building to check the place out before he moved into the president's office. I started thinking about waiting in the lobby and introducing myself when he came through the glass portico. And then on the appointed day, I actually did it.

Tuesday, 10:00 a.m. A big black Mercedes limo rolled into the driveway to the entry. A driver opened the door for his passenger.

"Excuse me, Mr. Bowen," I said, approaching the car. "I'm John Mason. I'm a contract lawyer. I'd love to spend ten minutes with you today."

"Okay, kid," he said without skipping a beat. "Come up to my office at one fifteen."

I was there exactly on time for what became a wonderful talk. I was able to ask him why he came to work in a limo. He cracked up.

"You know," he said, "I have so many drunk driving tickets, I don't have room for one more."

He became *my client* that day. Little did I know that Bowen's philosophy throughout his executive career was to fire all employees and ask them to formally apply for their old jobs. Clearly, I beat him to the punch that day and have been his attorney ever since. I think the shock of a "kid" asking such an impertinent question, combined with honesty and enthusiasm, led to his immediate decision to stick with me.

Over the years, Bowen became president of MCA Nashville (now owned by Universal), Warner Bros. Records, and Capitol Records, where he was instrumental in breaking the recording career of Garth Brooks. By the way, he tells me he fired everyone at all those companies, too, but brought 90 percent of them back within two weeks.

As the head of MCA, he produced George Strait and Reba McEntire, who was looking for new representation and a new MCA deal. Reba became a client of mine because Bowen told her to talk to me. It was the same for Conway Twitty.

3

A NEW LIFE

Meanwhile, a lawyer named Skip Brittenham, an eventual founding partner of Ziffren Brittenham, was in the small office next to mine at the Kaplan firm and also worked with television talent. His roster included Henry Winkler and a former construction worker known for building a good backyard deck from the Chicago suburbs who had promise. His name was Harrison Ford. Skip and I became friends, and I found him fascinating. He was a little older than I was and had done a tour with the air force. We had things in common, including the fact that we were part of a firm of seventy-one lawyers and knew that no matter how hard you worked or what money you brought in, you were stuck in a lockstep compensation system. This meant the founding partners basically made all the money. Of course, they did bring in most of it as well.

In 1977, Skip and I began to talk about how unfair this was to us. We were bringing in a million dollars each of billable hours to a firm that wanted to pay us $100,000 per year. We both asked for a raise to $250,000, which was good money in the '70s. We were elevated to partners and went to our first major meeting to talk about compensation, but the answer was no. I couldn't stand the politics, so I began to form a plan. Basically, I got Skip and a tax partner named David Gullen to agree to start our own law firm.

It made sense, and the three of us resigned. The other partners went berserk and took the position of "you can't quit, and if you do quit, you can't take any of your clients because they're the firm's clients. It's not fair or moral. We will turn you in to the California Bar and sue you as well." Funny thing: I thought becoming partner meant sharing in the profits. It didn't. It just meant going to meetings.

In the end, Skip and David backed out and decided to stay at the firm.

People supposed I wouldn't do it on my own, that I, too, would back down.

Instead, I started looking for office space.

With or without Skip and David, I would have left. And I made that clear to them. I had no doubt, as a confidant and warrior for my clients, that they would join me. I told the partners I would give them the first chance to speak with the clients, but that I had a right to tell them what I was doing and let them choose. That, by the way, is still the way it is in law firms, large and small.

All my clients, including Olivia Newton-John, Quincy Jones, Cat Stevens, and even the son-in-law of an important partner came with me. It wasn't long before I was also representing Donna Summer, Brian Wilson, Kenny Rogers, and Crystal Gayle. I knew I couldn't do all this work on my own and formed a partnership with another "loner" named Owen Sloane, who had left another big firm to represent artists and whose work I loved. His clients included Frank Zappa, Little River Band, and the duo Buckingham Nicks, soon to be the heart of Fleetwood Mac. (Years later, Owen negotiated a solo deal for Stevie Nicks with Modern Records. He went on vacation, so I had to go to her house to get the contract signed. Thankfully, I was able to answer all her questions and get her blue ink signature.)

I started the Law Offices of John Mason at 9200 Sunset Boulevard in Los Angeles on August 1, 1978. Soon, Mason & Sloane took off. It wasn't long before we were the go-to firm for major artists based in Los Angeles, Nashville, and Australia. We did great work by thinking outside the box. We were almost interchangeable in the sense that either one of us could step into the other's shoes with any client. Fortunately, one employee at the Kaplan firm came with me and was a big part of getting it started. We fell in love and were married in 1978. By 1984, we had had three beautiful girls. Sadly, despite and perhaps because of success and crazy lives, we separated and were divorced in 1985. We ended up friends and worked together to raise the girls, eventually working together on professional projects as well.

✦

In 1980, Owen and I added another solid music partner, Gary Gilbert. While he had some clients of his own, he was able to step into every deal for our main clients, so we could continue to grow. All of us felt there was little room for growth in music. We were at the top of our game and talked about attracting clients in film and television, but we knew from our experiences that the best way to do that was to bring in a star attorney with star clients. Norman Garey, a brilliant attorney who was also a part-time professor at Stanford Law School with about $10 million in billings and a client list that included the likes of Marlon Brando and Gene Hackman, would do.

The problem? He was a major partner in one of LA's biggest and best law firms in entertainment. No one believed he would leave to join a "music" firm, no matter how successful. He did and brought his clients with him. He also brought six film lawyers from his firm. In reality, the opportunity to build a new and powerful entertainment law firm with depth in music as well as television, film, and publishing was extremely compelling.

Building something new was our goal, but he had another one, which was to have his name go first. Deal!

We rented the top floor of a brand-new building on Ocean Avenue overlooking all of Santa Monica State Beach clear to Malibu. The rent was $50,000 a month, a staggering sum back then, but we could do it because the firm had an incredible client base and was on the verge of massive success.

If I learned one thing about show business, it is that the incredible highs are often accompanied by substantial lows. While Garey, Mason & Sloane was a huge success from day one, Norman apparently had huge problems with depression and perhaps schizophrenia. I'm no psychiatrist and never will know the facts, but on August 18, 1982, Norman shot himself at his house. His clients were incredibly distraught, while everyone in our firm was devastated to lose a partner and a friend.

I can only imagine the many things troubling Norman. However, one came to light dramatically over the following year. Early in our practice, Norman settled a lawsuit brought by Marlon Brando against Warner Bros. regarding his compensation in *Superman II*. Norman told us Brando was so happy with the result that he would pay our firm a $50,000 bonus. The check came in, and we all celebrated. About six months after Norman's death, Brando's new counsel sent a demand letter to our firm advising we had defaulted in repaying the $50,000 loan. We had never been advised the bonus was actually a loan. We were shocked to find that

Norman had actually signed a promissory note in the name of the firm and duped us into believing his claim. Brando ultimately sued Garey, Mason & Sloane, so this is a matter of public record. He ultimately, and generously, dismissed the claim and withdrew the lawsuit. Sadly, we found many more skeletons in the closet. However, that is not what this book is about.

It was a sad time in certain ways. Almost all his clients stayed with us, but that big rent started to look daunting. We worked harder and did well, but that didn't please everyone. My marriage fell apart. Luckily, the divorce was amicable, but I was suddenly a single father of three sharing custody fifty-fifty.

How am I going to do this? I thought. The answer was I met the love of my life, Bianca, in 1986. She was taking care of the kids of my close friends David Flynn and Jane Seymour. For me, it was love at first sight. She was twenty-one and I was thirty-six. Her interest in me back then was less than zero. I wasn't going to let that stop me and was happy when we began to go on a few dates.

Another silver lining was that Bianca and I became close friends with Morgan Mason (no relationship) and the singer Belinda Carlisle. Morgan is the son of the actor James Mason and his celebrity wife, Pamela. Belinda was the lead singer of the Go-Go's. We had a blast together and shared a lot of celebrity friends, both our own and the Hollywood gang who hung out with James and Pamela.

One night over dinner, we were talking about the best restaurants in LA and audaciously decided to open our own. "Mason's" was the logical name. We hired a corporate lawyer, raised the money, and opened the doors in 1986. We even hired the maître d' away from the Polo Lounge and the chef from the Hotel Bel-Air. It was the perfect celebrity hangout, as paparazzi weren't allowed and there was a wonderful outdoor patio, frequented regularly by Arnold Schwarzenegger and his cigar-smoking, bodybuilding friends. I can still see Dean Martin perched at the bar, sipping his ever-present chilled martini.

I will always remember opening night. We invited all the celebrities we knew, including the close friends of Morgan's parents. One of them, the actress Rue McClanahan, arrived in a beautiful new Jaguar. The next guest drove in behind her and gave the valet a big tip to "take care" of his car, a gleaming new Lamborghini Countach: stick shift, low slung, huge engine. The valet got in, starting the roaring engine, and drove it straight under Rue's Jag.

On another night not too long after this, Bianca and I were married on Mason's patio. All four of our parents were present. Jane Seymour was maid of honor, and Brian Wilson played piano. It was a beautiful, special day.

✦

By 1988, I felt it was time to move on in several ways. A month before our May 1988 wedding, I told Bianca I was done with LA and that I'd always wanted to live at Lake Tahoe. I hoped she felt the same way, and she did. The rest, including four more beautiful children, is history.

It was a fruitful time. Money was rolling in, and the names were getting bigger and bolder by the day.

4

BRIAN WILSON NEEDS HIS LIFE BACK

Something's wrong with me. I need your help.
—Brian Wilson

was fifteen years old when I met Brian Wilson for the first time in 1961. He was just nineteen, and the world stretched wide in front of both of us. This was back in my own band days leading the Vulcanes, when life was about gigs, rock and roll, and California vibes, dancing to our surf music. The show that night was in North Hollywood at a "venue" known as St. Charles Borromeo Catholic Church. We were the opening act for the Beach Boys.

We were all around the same age and music was our lives. That's where the similarities ended. They were huge. We weren't. However, we had a current hit, so the sock hop was packed. I remember arriving early that night after my dad dropped me off. (Yeah, that sort of does wreck the image of a rebellious rocker, but I didn't have wheels or a driver's license at age fifteen. Gas money was also questionable.) After finishing our set to polite applause, we slipped out the side door of the church, out on Lankershim Boulevard. The next act had rolled up, and there they were in their trademark Pendleton shirts and beige khakis, waiting in the cool night air in their station wagon (a real Woodie) with a surf-board on the roof.

Roll call: Brian Wilson, Mike Love, Dennis Wilson, Carl Wilson, and Al Jardine. They were the five founding members of the Beach Boys. Al jumped out of the car first, followed by the other guys. There were no roadies, just a bit of road to walk on as they carried their own instruments into the church. They opened their set with "Surfin' U.S.A." and the crowd went wild. I almost fainted! I'd *never* heard a band sound that good.

The kids in the audience were cool and danced to every song.

Brian Wilson played bass and sang lead back then. He had written "Surfin' U.S.A.," "Surfin' Safari," and a bunch of other simple songs with complex harmonies. He was not a performer and seemed pained to be standing up there in front of a crowd. Mike Love and Dennis Wilson were on fire and made the girls go wild.

After the show, we said hello; they nodded. You didn't need much more in those days than music to form a bond—an unspoken one—that linked you. We were musicians; they were destined to become international superstars.

I ran into Brian a few times back in 1962 and 1963. We shared things about our bands. He had formed the Beach Boys with his brothers, Carl and Dennis, plus cousin Mike and friend Al, in 1961. He told me how his band was run by his father, Murry, who was also a songwriter, talent manager, and record producer. Brian said they were just trying to make good music while having fun. He had no idea why they were having such huge success. But I knew when I listened from backstage in the church that they were incredible. Here were five guys playing on a makeshift stage in the gym of a church, and they were groundbreaking, drawing on 1950s rock and roll music and mixing in some R&B to create their unique vocal harmonies set to the themes of teenage love and other adventures. Later, the little family group with the California sound would go on to challenge the Beatles as the greatest band on the planet.

Back then, Brian was just a shy young guy, not particularly engaging. Especially at those early shows, he was just a singer and a musician in a new surf band. But not only was he the lead singer, producer, and songwriter of the Beach Boys, but he was actually a musical genius decades ahead of his time who would go on to do groundbreaking work. Who knew?

Brian just didn't have the personality for live music stardom. Turns out, he didn't really want to be a performer, and eventually, he freaked out and had a nervous breakdown. Some blamed it on him "frying his brain" with drugs. Others said it had to do with childhood trauma and rumors of physical and verbal abuse from Murry, which his father always quickly denied but which Brian always confirmed. Honestly, he seemed "troubled" every time I saw him. Many times, over the years, he said, "John, I just fried my brain. I took too many drugs."

By 1968, Brian quit performing and devoted himself to songwriting. His mission was "to make the greatest music," and that quest continued as his mental health declined. He eventually became so bizarre that he would sit at the piano in his living room surrounded by actual sand that had been dumped in big piles in a sort of playpen.

He was forsaking his young family—wife Marilyn, a singer with the group the Honeys, and young kids Carnie and Wendy— for his strange kind of creative peace. Four years passed, and he never left the house. His weight ballooned to 350 pounds from eating entire birthday cakes as a late-night snack. Marilyn was devastated and enlisted the other Beach Boys to help save Brian's life.

Marilyn eventually brought in a counterculture psychologist named Eugene Landy who was known for his unconventional twenty-four-hour therapy and treatment of celebrities. Landy would become both famous and infamous, and Brian would become his most well-known client. Brian found something magical and mystical in him.

That day, Brian walked into a room in his home and found Marilyn talking in person with Landy. Brian approached him and reportedly said, "Something's wrong with me. I need your help."

Later, Brian would say that the only reason he accepted Landy was to avoid being committed to a psychiatric hospital.

Marilyn hired Landy in October 1975 in an attempt to find someone who could deal with Brian, who had refused to attend appointments with psychiatrists and therapists. Landy diagnosed Brian as an "undiagnosed and untreated schizophrenic." However, he was a therapist and not a psychiatrist, which would become a big problem later on.

✦

Brian improved in many ways under Landy's supervision and control, but he also formed a controversial business and creative partnership with Landy. I say this not from experience but from common knowledge. I never saw Brian during that time, but I did stay in touch with his brother Carl, who was the same age as me and went to a nearby high school. On the plus side, Brian lost a tremendous amount of weight by eating only healthy foods and exercising daily. However, he was completely controlled by Landy and his handlers.

Brian was also not allowed to speak with his family, even his daughters, or anyone in the band. Mike, Carl, Al, and even Bruce Johnston, who had replaced Brian in the band, could not accept his isolation. Finally, the band's manager, Tom Hulett, stepped in and suggested Brian needed a strong, independent balance to the Landy team. Tom and the guys thought I would be perfect. I was already known to the Beach Boys, especially to Mike and Carl, who called all the shots now.

My reputation for independence and integrity was verifiable. It was why Brian Wilson walked into my office, then on Sunset Boulevard in West Los Angeles, with Landy back in 1986. I was surprised that Brian was not the same guy physically whom I had known and performed with in the '60s. And he was certainly not the same guy in any way emotionally. For sure, his experiments with drugs, especially LSD and cocaine, had diminished his mental capacity, but it was clear from the day he came in that Brian was controlled by prescription drugs and what I call the "Landy handlers." The Landy handlers were all nice, but they secretly or openly recorded everything Brian and anyone else said so Landy and his team could evaluate what was going on and control Brian's follow-up.

✦

The business of being a Beach Boy was another matter, and Landy wanted to insert himself into that part of Brian's life.

From the outset of my relationship with Landy, he dreamed of getting Brian back the ownership of his songs. We talked and talked about how Brian's father, Murry, had pushed and forced Brian and even Mike to sell their ownership in all the Beach Boys' hits. Murry, of course, got a big commission. Ultimately, I decided to go the route of unwinding the sale on the basis that Brian did not have the mental capacity to understand or make the sale.

In 1981, I said, "We should be able to get the songs back." There was no statute of limitations for fraud in those days. Brian would have to sue Almo, and we banked on Brian's disability to help us. We also banked on the fraud theory. Almo/Irving Music defrauded Brian. Almo was buying Brian's songs from his father and manager, who didn't own them. None of this was in his son's best interest or even legally possible.

Meanwhile, Brian did not have the mental capacity to make important business decisions. It was a clear case of incapacity, meaning he didn't have the ability to do certain things including manage his own affairs. If you have incapacity, there is no statute of limitations, meaning it can't run out. You are not held responsible for your decisions.

I brought in a litigator and filed an action on Brian's behalf. Landy was ecstatic. There was no way the other side could win on incapacity. There wasn't one document that Brian Wilson signed with knowledge of the transaction. He didn't know what was happening. He played piano in a sandbox.

The purchaser fought back hard, but in the end, Brian won back all his songs and walked away clean from this heinous deal. But Mike Love had also started saying that Brian didn't write some of the songs alone. Mike sued, and Brian agreed Mike was the cowriter of many of the past hits, including "California Girls."

Brian owns his share of them to this day.

✦

As for Brian's business relationship with the Beach Boys, let's say it was complicated.

First, back to the old days: Way back in the '60s, founding member Al Jardine left the group to go to dental school. While he was away, the group, perhaps at the urging of Murry, set up Brother Records, Inc. (BRI). It was their sole entity for recordings and live performances. Al was denied his share because he'd left, even though he came back to the Beach Boys less than a year later and stayed until he was kicked out by a majority vote in the '90s. When I came on board in 1985, BRI not only still existed (and still does today), but it had regular shareholder meetings where members would vote on everything, including concert dates, new albums, etc. The band's manager, Tom Hulett, would present what was on the table.

By the time I got involved, Brian hadn't toured with the group in decades, but he still had his vote, as did all the founding members except for Al. Likewise, Brian's replacement during tours, Bruce Johnston, a critical part of the Beach Boys to this day, had no share, no votes, no say. He wasn't invited to the meetings. Dennis Wilson had drowned, and his widow gave her proxy to her brother-in-law Carl. Mike, Carl, and Brian had 100 percent of the shares, but Carl effectively had 50 percent, with Brian and Mike at 25 percent each.

Brian was still treated with the utmost respect during meetings. When I look back, Landy did not ever try to interfere with the votes or try to tell Brian what to do in a meeting, though a handler was always there to record every meeting and every word. Often, Landy would call me the next day after a meeting to ask why I "let" Brian vote the way he did. I would always say, "That is what he felt."

Once I became Brian's attorney, maybe because my office was big enough, all the meetings (generally monthly) were held there. What a crowd! Each member of the band brought an attorney and an accountant to the meetings, including Al Jardine. Even though he had no vote, nevertheless, as a founder, he came to all meetings and brought his own team. Votes were held on everything at every meeting. Mike was ultimately able to secure proxies from the widows and heirs of Carl and Dennis, giving him 75 percent voting rights, which ultimately led to Landy's termination.

Landy had every meeting recorded and frequently got Brian to not only change his votes after the fact but also to lobby his brothers and their representatives to change their votes as well. Of course, although there were more than a few occasions where Brian "decided" to change his vote, it rarely mattered, as 90 percent of all votes were unanimous.

For every meeting, I set up concentric circles of chairs in my large corner office with the Beach Boys in the center and their various advisers and the Landy handler right behind them in a second row. Everything actually functioned smoothly for years, even with changing votes and issues. I have to say that Brian always participated, and it is important to remember that the Landy twenty-four-hour therapy brought Brian out of a literal sandbox in his living room to a productive personal, business, and musical life. It was beautiful to hear stories, schedule tours, and listen to new songs and plans for recording them. Just listen to Brian's song "Love and Mercy" for a beautiful taste of where he was back then. However, I digress. The music and beyond came with a strict program.

Landy had a big ego and soon took control of every aspect of Brian's life. He tried to control the Beach Boys as well but ran up against a brick wall with cousin Mike and brother Carl, who also had Dennis's heirs' votes when they needed them. At home, Landy believed in a routine of exercise and productivity. Friends and family deemed by Landy as a negative influence were banned from visiting or spending time with Brian.

All this control came with a price. Landy's monthly fee was extravagant and rose by 200 percent as time went by.

The good news was Brian lost 150 pounds and lived, proving to Landy that his program worked.

But at what cost?

Brian was also put on meds at Landy's direction, which was preposterous because Landy was a PhD and not a medical doctor. He could not prescribe medicine. He had to "consult" with real doctors to get that done—and he did. There was psychotherapy and the aforementioned exercise in the mix. By the mid-1980s, Landy insisted that he influenced "all of [Brian Wilson's] thinking. I'm practically a member of the band." Brian refuted that, insisting, "People say that Dr. Landy runs my life, but the truth is, I'm in charge." Brian was not in charge.

Landy claimed that Brian could go anywhere he wanted on his own but "chose" not to do that. Eventually, part of Landy's program included removing Brian's contact with the band, which cost him the opportunity to cowrite and perform the hit "Kokomo." But more on that in a minute.

I wasn't intimidated by Landy. Much of the time he truly had Brian's best interest in mind and kept him healthy physically and functioning. But Landy wanted 100 percent control over Brian. He realized that he couldn't make that kind of money anywhere else except with Brian, who had become his obsession.

I couldn't support Landy's total control and insisted on meeting regularly with Brian alone along with the many meetings I had with Brian and Landy together. Brian was generally there physically but not mentally. It was normal for him not to remember what he'd said in the last meeting or even an hour ago.

I believe that Brian didn't care about what the Beach Boys did at this point. He was happy in his beach house and with being a hermit who earned enough money to live well and allow his family the means to live well. Brian was the least likely of the Wilson brothers to live in the past and least likely to be alive today in 2025. Funny how it all works out.

There was a consistent rhythm for years during which Brian could be himself within Landy's universe of control—until 1990, when Landy decided he needed yet more money and yet more power. All of a sudden, he raised his fee and wanted cowriter credit on all of Brian's new songs. I didn't believe that was fair.

There was also a major missed opportunity. In 1987, Mike brought the Beach Boys the opportunity to write and record the main song for the movie *Cocktail*, starring Tom Cruise. Landy refused to let Brian participate unless he was a writer on the song, too. Mike, Carl, and Bruce refused and went on to write and record "Kokomo," the biggest Beach Boys hit in decades, without Brian's input. I'm sure Brian regrets that to this day. When Mike played the song for us in a BRI meeting, we all knew it would be a smash. For me, the fact that Landy insisted on being fifty-fifty equals with Brian Wilson was the last straw.

This marked a new era for the band. "Kokomo" was a massive worldwide hit, as it captured the old sound but remained fresh at the same time. This clearly indicated the Beach Boys were more than just the words and the music of Brian Wilson. What was best for the group now trumped what was best for Brian. At the same time, family and friends pushed for Landy's ouster. When

Landy left for the first time, Brian fell into a serious depression, so he was hired back.

In my opinion, by 1989, Landy wasn't concerned with what was best for the group or Brian. He wanted only what was best for himself, which meant big tours making tons of money. Brian didn't want to be a Beach Boy anymore. He wanted to be a producer and songwriter. He also truly wanted to be well. Carl gave a lot of input in those days. I found him to be a sweet guy and a fantastic singer, songwriter, and musician who really cared about the members of the band. It was Mike who decided to kick Al Jardine out.

After Carl died of lung cancer, Mike, with the support of Carl's and Dennis's widows, had 75 percent control of everything. He took a stand. He told Brian, "You're so controlled by Landy that the rest of us will now outvote you on everything."

Through all of it—the highs and the lows, the drugs and the fog—Brian still did what he did best: He wrote songs. In fact, when I married my beloved Bianca, Brian decided, along with Landy and Landy's girlfriend, Alexandra Morgan, to write us a song. Brian made the record and performed it at our wedding at Mason's restaurant. We still have the original recording of "John and Bianca's Wedding." It's awesome. Brian is truly a giant teddy bear and genius who regrets bad decisions and lives for better ones.

Landy, incidentally, was now earning huge fees and claiming to write every song with Brian. Again, I remember asking to meet with Brian regularly alone in my office. Unfortunately, Brian reported everything I said to Landy. Some of the meetings were even recorded. The time came in 1990 when I told Landy it was either him or me. I told him I would call Brian to give him the choice.

"Go ahead," he said.

"So, Brian," I began, "you hired me to be your lawyer and I am. But I can't be your lawyer if you're under the control of Landy. You agree to things and then he changes your mind.

"You're losing all of this money," I added. "If you don't fire Landy, I will have to resign."

"Okay," Brian said, "I'll go talk to Eugene."

Next day, my phone rings.

"How dare you have a meeting with Brian!" Landy fumed. "How dare you tell him I'm taking advantage!"

"I'm out," I said.

It was no surprise that Brian said, "I have to stay with Eugene."

✦

By the time Brian divorced Marilyn, he was still living with Landy, who had moved into Brian's house. Brian had also met Melinda Ledbetter, who was destined to become Mrs. Wilson and mother of five adopted children.

The scorecard: Melinda was in, and she wanted Landy out. Landy could fire me, but he couldn't make Brian dump her, although he tried. Landy ordered Brian again and again to dump her. The icon didn't exactly listen and continued the relationship.

The end was finally in sight when Mike's and Brian's families sued Landy and got him legally removed and ultimately his license in California revoked. This happened after it was estimated that between 1983 and 1991, Landy earned millions from Brian. At the same time, astute Melinda went to court and helped Wilson serve Landy with a 1991 court order barring him from any contact with the Beach Boy.

Melinda also thankfully led Brian toward proper medical care. By 1999, she would take over Brian's business management, keeping things honest and watching out for Brian's best interests. When Melinda passed away in 2024, Brian was placed in a conservatorship to protect his health, business, and legacy.

✦

Writing this chapter, I remembered well an interview I did with Diane Sawyer in October 1991 for *Primetime Live*. Diane reported on Brian's troubles over thirty years. She focused on his family and friends' lawsuit to remove Landy from Brian's life. Landy actually agreed to be interviewed, I suppose to gain public support. At a heated point in the interview, Diane asked Landy, "Can anyone actually reach Brian Wilson by phone?"

"Yes," Landy answered, "his attorney, John Mason."

On camera for national television, I denied the allegation, because every call I ever had with Brian was routed first through a handler, who then sought Landy's approval, and *only* then would he alert Brian that he needed to come to the phone. When that stage was set, I finally spoke with Brian. Each of those calls was monitored and recorded and followed the next day by Brian's explanations, clarifications, and even denials after his briefing with Landy.

A fun anecdote regarding that interview revolves around Diane Sawyer, one of the greatest television journalists of all time. Diane and her producer Shelley Ross came to my oceanside office in Santa Monica. The crew set up the camera and lights, putting two chairs across from each other. Diane walked in, looked across at me with a big smile, and said, "Would you mind if I put some of my pancake on your head? It will really make the glow from the sun softer on your head."

"Of course," I said.

She reached into her purse, pulled out her own pancake makeup, and applied it to my bald head.

That story and interview are still up on YouTube.

✦

Gradually, Brian began to tour and completed his 2004 album, *Smile*, with all-new recordings of music that he originally created. He credited Melinda with helping him resume his career, including the Beach Boys' fiftieth anniversary reunion tour, which involved all surviving members. The tour ended before it was supposed to finish. Some blamed Melinda. Mike Love has made it known that he was disappointed that he wasn't allowed to collaborate with Brian on the 2012 Beach Boys album produced by Brian called *That's Why God Made the Radio*. He said that he was promised. He also accused Melinda of installing an Auto-Tune unit on each of the other band members' microphones. Mike and Melinda didn't get along, leading to her banishment from rehearsals until the tour ended.

Melinda had the last word in 2014: A good portion of the Brian Wilson biopic *Love & Mercy* was written from her point of view, with Elizabeth Banks playing her. Ironically, it was Landy and Brian who came up with the concept and title.

Speaking of Landy, thrice divorced, he spent his post–Brian Wilson years in psychotherapeutic practice, with licenses only in New Mexico and Hawaii, until his death of pneumonia and lung cancer at age seventy-one in Honolulu. When told of Landy's death, Brian commented, "I was devastated." Later Brian admitted, "I thought he was my friend, but he was a very fucked-up man. I still feel that there was benefit. I try to overlook the bad stuff, and be thankful for what he taught me."

It came out in the press that Landy didn't exactly tell the truth about the drugs Brian was on during the days when Landy controlled him. Yes, they were prescribed by a psychiatrist and licensed physicians, but Landy "advised" these people. They prescribed what Landy wanted.

The cocktail of substances made Brian far more controllable. The cocktail also meant he could perform and seem normal. Most of the time, he was too weak and out of it to defend himself. At one point, Landy wouldn't allow Brian to talk to Marilyn or his daughters Carnie and Wendy, which was just the lowest.

I never accepted that, and it cost me my relationship with Brian.

Most people would have died from taking that many drugs, but he's still alive. His two younger, healthier brothers are gone: Carl was a lifelong smoker; Dennis fell off a boat. Mike is in his eighties and still out there performing and mentally astute. Mike could control it. Brian never could. It left him a shell of himself.

Still, Brian was with Melinda for over twenty years, and he welcomes all his children to his home. He makes millions a year with the oldies and gets his share of any Beach Boy performances owned by Brothers Records. I have seen Brian many times since 1990, including on stage and in person. Little has changed. The 2021 documentary *Brian Wilson: Long Promised Road* sheds light on his insecurities and the damage done from drugs, prescribed and not, and the paternal abuse that might or might not have happened.

To me, he was always a kind, thoughtful, and generous man. He remains a creature of habit. For decades he ate at the same café where we used to meet when I represented him. We've met there from time to time to talk about the old days, about what he remembers from the '60s, when a big show was done on a Friday night in a high school gym or church.

He is still and always will be Brian Wilson—a genius!

5

Q UNFILTERED

The thing is . . . dreams are infectious.
—Quincy Jones

n 1966, I was in my second year at UCLA. My band was offered a lounge gig for a weekend in Las Vegas. Guess they didn't check IDs back in the day. We did the early show, then went over to the legendary Sands Hotel to catch the late set of the Chairman of the Board, Frank Sinatra. The Copa Room was filled with blue smoke, smelled boozy like gin and red wine, and had that Vegas sizzle where just about anything could happen. Someone cut the lights. Total darkness. The announcer said the magic words: "Live from the Sands, it's Frank Sinatra!"

It's hard to imagine the Copa today, especially after Frank performed in only sold-out arenas for decades, but the Copa showroom in the Sands had a seating capacity of just 385. It is even harder to imagine entertainers like Frank playing two shows a night six days a week, plus a Sunday afternoon matinee. All you can do to get an idea of what it was like to be there is listen to the many live albums recorded at the Copa, including *Sinatra at the Sands*. Still, those records cannot capture the magic of the live Count Basie Orchestra, conducted by Quincy Jones, on stage with Frank in front of all 385 of us lucky enough to get in. Think of it: a dinner show (without good food) with waiters, servers, busboys, cigarette girls, and photographers all wandering around, smoke filling the room (we didn't know better back then). When Quincy cranked up the band and Frank walked onstage, nothing else mattered.

Watching Frank perform (and drink) just a few yards away was incredible. Hands down, it was one of the best shows I have ever seen in my life because of those legendary vocals and the explosive, swinging Count Basie band that made it seem like the seats would unhinge and float into the air. You know live music is great when it's almost an out-of-body experience. Sinatra's was that kind of show. Heart soaring. Jaw dropping. Memories sealed in my personal time capsule.

But even the best of the best don't get there alone. Later I found out that the music was all Quincy. He was the arranger and conductor for the shows at the Sands and during the sold-out, critically acclaimed nationwide tour that followed. He later did those huge arrangements for such artists as Louis Armstrong, Sarah Vaughan, and Ray Charles. And there he stood with Frank, right in front of the band. The guy was side by side with Frank for years—and talked to Ol' Blue Eyes until the day the icon died. Quincy Jones would go on to make an indelible mark on the entire music industry, as well as my life.

I didn't know much about Quincy in those early days, but I still thought, *Man, that guy is super cool*. And when I met him briefly backstage at the 1972 Grammy Awards, I added "charming" and "mesmerizing" to the list.

Quincy Delight Jones Jr. (Q to his friends) was born on the South Side of Chicago in 1933. His mother was a bank officer and apartment complex manager, while his father, Quincy Sr., was a semiprofessional baseball player turned carpenter. In high school, Q decided to carve his own path. He took music lessons and developed brilliant skills as a trumpeter and arranger. He went to Garfield High with Charlie Taylor, who played sax, and they joined forces. By age fourteen, Quincy had introduced himself to then-sixteen-year-old Ray Charles after sneaking in to watch him at the Black Elks Club in Chicago. A love of music burned in Q, as it did in me at that age.

Q had that certain something. He was a genius and had a heavy dose of magnetism. He was loved by everyone, including Count Basie, Sinatra, and Martin Luther King Jr. Back in the day, he was a working man who juggled as many good opportunities as possible. I began to notice his name announcing projects. Q toured as a trumpet player for Lionel Hampton and went from there to Mercury Records, where he was the first Black vice president of a white record company. Q was also hired by the film director Sidney Lumet to score the movie *The Pawnbroker*.

It was just the beginning of a stunning career that spanned more than seventy years in the entertainment industry, with eighty Grammy nominations, twenty-eighty Grammy wins, and a Grammy Legend Award in 1992. Q also produced Michael Jackson's biggest albums, including *Off the Wall*, *Thriller*, and *Bad*.

✦

It was during my Kaplan days in the mid-'70s that I really got to know Q. It was through my newest, but still senior, colleague Harold Lipton, a corporate lawyer who'd moved from New York to Los Angeles. The last name might sound familiar. Harold was the father of the actress Peggy Lipton, who played Julie Barnes on *The Mod Squad*, which was one of the most popular TV series from 1968 to 1973. She moved on from the series to marry Q in 1974. The union would last until 1990 and produce two beautiful daughters, Kidada and Rashida, who also went into show business.

It was Harold Lipton who told Q, "I have this great lawyer at my firm. You should meet John Mason." It wasn't long before I was driving to Quincy and Peggy's gorgeous home in Bel Air, thinking, *Oh my, I'm going to meet Peggy and Quincy. This will be a pretty good day.*

So there I am, driving through what looks like the set for *Lifestyles of the Rich and Famous*. I was buzzed in at the gate and drove up to the house. The maid let me in, and I found a super low-key Q waiting for me at a small, round table in the nook of their family kitchen, illuminated by brilliant California sunlight. He had just married Peggy a few months before, and their baby had already been born. The idea was we would have breakfast, and soon I found myself sipping freshly squeezed OJ out of a crystal glass in this beautiful home.

I was twenty-eight, impressionable, and looking at a dream life. Those were the days when I was more awestruck by material things, and Q and Peggy had the best of the best. I hadn't really been around this sort of elevated lifestyle much in my life, although my band often played in private homes in Beverly Hills and Bel Air. I was just never invited back for breakfast.

Q was just super cool from the start. We talked about how he had produced Lesley Gore's big hits "It's My Party" and the classic "You Don't Own Me," as well as his work with Frank Sinatra. All that fell away when the wonderful and charming Peggy walked into the room barefoot and in sweatpants, no makeup and stick-straight, perfect California blond hair. She had a baby girl on her hip and love in her eyes for her genius husband. Peggy nursed the baby and then made us tea and breakfast.

There was an instant connect between all three of us. Or four, if you count the baby Kidada, whom I held in my arms while Peggy poured the tea. That day in 1974, Q hired me, and from there we did it all together: record deals, movie deals, and everything else that happened in between. The common thread was that if you were around Q, you were going to be successful. He was real with big dreams. Q would say, "The thing is . . . dreams are infectious." So were his smile and laugh.

That day, Q told me exactly what he wanted to do: start his own music publishing and record companies. He was done with being an employee for hire or an arranger of work that already existed. It was almost destined that Quincy would strike out on his own, because there were no bosses in his life. There were no limits. But as his lawyer, I found that when it came to business, Q was not a detail guy. Of course, he didn't need too much in that department. Above all, he just wanted to trust someone to take care of it. And that's how we worked. He started things, and I helped execute them.

All these lofty aspirations almost never happened.

In 1974, Q was busy working when he collapsed. Later, he would say that it felt like a shotgun was fired inside his head. He was rushed to the hospital, where he was diagnosed with a brain aneurysm, or a weakness in the main artery to the brain that caused it to pop. What followed was a seven-and-a-half-hour operation where doctors discovered a second aneurysm that was ready to blow, and another operation was scheduled.

It was a horrible time and most men would have died—that is, most men who are not Quincy Jones. Even Q would say that "it didn't look too promising, to the point that my friends planned a memorial service for me at the Shrine Auditorium in LA."

We were all praying for his recovery, and Quincy pulled out of it. You could see the scar on his forehead from the operations, but he returned to 100 percent with one caveat: Docs would no long allow him to play the trumpet because of metal implants.

Q attended what was supposed to be his funeral but turned into a big party for him, with friends showing up including Sidney Poitier, Sarah Vaughan, and on and on. Q would later say that the health scare taught him that you can't sit around feeling sorry for yourself. He had a one in a hundred chance of surviving, but he didn't let that get him down. "If I sat around feeling sorry for myself, I would have never gone on to do *Thriller*, 'We Are the World,' or *The Color Purple*," he said.

We had breakfast at his home once a month and talked by phone at least once a day. I'm sure Q slept sometimes, but you wouldn't know from his work schedule and the many events he attended. When he asked me to make his artist deal at A&M Records with Herb Alpert, who deferred the details to Jerry Moss, I was taken aback because I knew he could no longer play the trumpet. (Coincidentally, Herb was also a trumpet player with many hit records to his credit.) Q told me not to worry. He could make the records without playing on them. His arrangements and productions with singers and musicians he hired would be the basis for his huge "solo" albums *The Dude*, *Sounds . . . and Stuff Like That!!*, and *Body Heat*.

"Trust me, man," he said. "Herbie gets it, and I can make it happen."

Notwithstanding his success at A&M (Alpert and Moss), it was the legendary record executive Mo Ostin at Warner/Reprise who believed enough to give Q his own label, Qwest Records. Being a lawyer for artists, I had never made a deal for an artist on one label (A&M) and a deal for the same artist with a different label (Warner/Reprise) for the development of other artists, who would actually be signed exclusively to a third label (Qwest).

"Don't worry," Q said. "I've already got the talent."

Our work included me helping set up Qwest as a joint venture with Warner Bros. Records. Qwest ended up giving the world classics like George Benson's *Give Me the Night*, Patti Austin's *Every Home Should Have One*, and the Brothers Johnson's "Strawberry Letter 23." He always picked the most talented people to work with him. That was a big part of his success. The other parts: smarts and hustle. Quincy was so happy with my contract work during those days that he gave me personal gold records for Michael Jackson's *Off the Wall*, the Brothers Johnson, Patti Austin, James Ingram, and more. I still have them.

With extraordinary artists came hit after hit. Qwest was an instant success and a rare label where nearly everything was both a hit and a quality product. Q hired the son of Billy Eckstine (Ed Eckstine), a longtime friend, to head the label. He was a great leader from the start and became a friend as well. The company focused on R&B, but Q also branched out with some eclectic signings, including the British new wave band New Order and the gospel group the Winans. He also ventured into hip-hop before Qwest shut down in 2000.

For years, Q would call nearly every day with a new brilliant idea. I was just crazy lucky to put his ideas on paper and to get paid for it as well. It didn't surprise me when Q came with me when I broke away from the Kaplan firm. It did surprise and hurt his father-in-law, who believed in the old-school concept that all clients belong to the firm and shouldn't have loyalty to lawyers who work there. Sadly, Harold Lipton, a wonderful man, never spoke to me again.

✦

In 1978, Q called to tell me that Michael Jackson had asked him to produce his first solo album, which turned out to be *Off the Wall*.

Michael had, by then, begun searching for his own lawyers, so I made the deal for Q with Michael's manager, Freddy DeMann. It was a terrific deal for Q and Michael to do three albums together. They were all hugely successful, and lots of money was made by all. However, when Michael came up short for cash, his advisers cut off royalties to Q and DeMann. Both of them sued and got much of what they deserved in the first place. The contract I did for Q stood the test of time and changed technology (all too often, the "business" doesn't change with it). The deal and contract I put together for Q with Michael had the standard "superstar producer" royalty of 5 percent of the suggested retail list price (SRLP), but it also included rights to participate in income from audiovisual use of the master recordings and rights to produce edits and remixes. (That being said, I was not involved in the lawsuits and have no opinion on how they turned out.)

Being around Q also meant traveling in lofty circles and hearing stories about the people who gravitated toward him. He knew everyone from John F. Kennedy to the author Alex Haley, who wrote *Roots*. I remember Q telling me that *Roots* on television was going to be huge, although a long-form show about black families wasn't the norm at the time. Q just knew because he had an amazing gut feeling for talent and integrity. He introduced me to Haley, who signed a copy of his book for me. He wrote: "To the family of John Mason from the family of Kunta Kinte." It remains one of my prized possessions.

In the end, clients and lawyers move on for a variety of reasons. I remember being invited by Q for breakfast at the Hotel Bel-Air before he did the music for Steven Spielberg's *The Color Purple*, starring a young Oprah Winfrey. I thought it would be another of our special and productive meetings, but when I sat down, his first words were a surprise.

"I have to move on, John. I need Spielberg's lawyer," he told me. "I gotta go."

"Did you bring me here to fire me?" I asked.

"Well, I wouldn't put it that way," he said.

The result was the same.

I said, with tears in my eyes and running down my cheeks, "Q, if you are firing me, I need to leave."

I stood up, gave him a hug (a Q tradition), and walked out into the perfect California weather to get into my car.

The valet saw my tears and asked, "Are you okay?"

Of course I said yes as I pulled myself together.

I was devasted. I remember Ed Eckstine trying to console me: "Don't worry, man, Quincy is a chameleon." It was nothing personal, he was trying to tell me. Later, Ed would be let go as well.

✦

Q was twelve years older than me, and so he'd always figured as an older brother in my life, sometimes disappointing me, but always trying to support and guide me.

"I gotta tell you, man," he began one day. "Here's the story of how I feel about life. There are two bulls up on a hill. They see a herd of cows down in the valley. The young bull says to the old bull, 'Let's go down there and fuck one of those cows.' The old bull says, 'No, let's go down there and fuck all of those cows.'"

That was Q: always patient, always thinking there would be more and better opportunities, always maximizing every one that came to him, always knowing the future was still far away. And that was still where he was at, even in his nineties.

We still talked after I was let go, about wives, kids, and crazy times. He truly loved Peggy, with whom he shared a beautiful relationship. It did end, and I wasn't around for that part. I do think she probably just got burned out with all the hangers-on and people around him. It was a wonderful life while it lasted. She didn't act much after they married and preferred to be a great mom. Later, she gave up on the lifestyle. I can tell you that when Peggy died, Q was as broken up as a man could ever be about a woman. He still loved her and always wished that he hadn't messed things up between them. Sure, there were other women after Peggy, including Natasha Kinski, but he still loved Peggy. If you ask me, Q could love many people. That was just him. I am happy to be one. He certainly adored Frank Sinatra. They were so close and spoke every single day until the day Frank was gone. Quincy would tell stories about going out with Frank and getting drunk enough to be physically thrown out of a place.

The guy remained ageless even at ninety. Q could still be involved in ten things at one time. And he was a man of strong convictions. One time he went off the deep end and told me that the Beatles weren't so good, in his opinion. The guy said stuff like that. He was unfiltered. We had a heated debate about it for what felt like hours.

"How could you say the Beatles aren't talented?" I demanded.

"I didn't say *that* exactly, but they're not *that* good."

And on and on.

All I can say is that the guy was magical and I loved that about him.

At least once a month, even though I still had to go through his answering service, I'd ring him and then hear, "Who may I say is calling Mr. Jones?" He always came on the line, no matter what he was doing. He was always busy, still running the show, including Quincy Jones Productions and Quincy Jones Music Publishing. It was tough just keeping up with him. His success and his drive couldn't be matched. Neither could his charm and genius.

We hugged when we would see each other—and remember when.

One last thing, Q: The Beatles were damn good. I wish you were here to debate.

6

ROY ORBISON SINGS FOR THE LONELY

My voice is a gift. This life is a gift.
—Roy Orbison

In 1963, the opening act on the Roy Orbison UK tour was . . . the Beatles! Not half bad for a twenty-seven-year-old, but Roy wasn't just your average guy. He had already written and recorded a slew of hit records, including "Ooby Dooby," "Only the Lonely (Know the Way I Feel)," "Crying," "Dream Baby (How Long Must I Dream)," and "In Dreams." A year later, he would release "Oh, Pretty Woman."

When the tour was over, Roy came back to Nashville and learned the love of his life and the mother of their three sons, Claudette, wanted a divorce. He was devastated but wouldn't give up on his "dream" wife and life. They reconciled ten months later and married again in 1965. Sadly, on June 6, 1966, while riding motorcycles together in Gallatin, Tennessee, Claudette hit a pickup truck that had turned in front of her bike and died on the road in his arms.

All of a sudden, he lost it all. His records were no longer hitting, but he could still pack a house in England. While on tour there in 1968, Roy learned his home back in Tennessee had burned down and his two older sons had died in the flames. I still choke up thinking of these tragedies.

After that, Roy's pale skin, black clothing, and dark glasses could be seen as a manifestation of his grief, but these famous characteristics had roots in his childhood. Previously, he had worn the glasses because he suffered terrible stage fright. And even earlier, as a kid born in Vernon, Texas, the middle son of a nurse and an oil-well driller and mechanic named Orbie, he wore those clunky midnight-colored glasses to completely hide. All the kids in the Orbison family had terrible vision, and Roy grew up wearing thick corrective lenses. Self-conscious and shy, he dyed his almost white childhood hair black to fit in.

He found his calling the day Orbie gave him a guitar as a birth-day present. His father taught him the chords to "You Are My Sunshine." All of a sudden, Roy was practicing day and night while also winning all the local talent shows. He sang rockabilly and country as a teenager, forming a band with some friends called the Wink Westerners. They played Glenn Miller songs and country music at local bars and honky-tonks. Roy enrolled in North Texas State College to study geology (as his backup career). But when his pal Pat Boone signed a record deal, he recommitted himself to music.

Roy played with his band on local TV, which led friends to insist that Roy audition for Sam Phillips, who personally signed him to Sun Records. Sam had already signed and broke Elvis Presley, Johnny Cash, and Jerry Lee Lewis. The singer took his first royalties and made a down payment on a Cadillac.

It was a dream life . . . until it wasn't.

After the string of horrible luck and loss, Roy tried to move on. In 1969, he married a German teenage fan, Barbara Wellhoener

Jacobs, who first met Roy in 1968 when she was just seventeen and he was thirty-two. It was two years after the tragic death of Claudette. They had two sons together, but neither Roy nor Barbara lived happily for many years.

In 1973, Roy was hurting. He didn't own his masters or his songs, and he had been dropped by his label, MGM Records. My friend Mike Curb had been president of MGM and signed Roy to a decent contract, but when Mike left the label, the new president decided to drop most of Mike's artists, including Roy. When Mike heard, he told Roy to call me, and he did.

It was 1978. I had just left the Kaplan firm to strike out on my own. Even with Olivia Newton-John, Quincy Jones, Donna Summer, and Cat Stevens as clients, the thought of working with Roy was exciting. I had rented an office suite at 200 Sunset Boulevard—literally on the famed Sunset Strip—and recently bought a house in Brentwood. I felt empowered to work with legends and to right the decades of unfair deals extracted from talent. Roy was both a legend and someone who had been totally taken advantage of.

Roy was staying at the Beverly Hilton, so we agreed to have a breakfast meeting there. Wow, going to breakfast with Roy Orbison was like a dream come true. I had no idea back then what he had been through, personally and in business. When I got there, he was sitting alone at a small table in the coffee shop with just a cup of coffee.

"I am pleased to meet you, Mr. Mason," he said. "I hope you can help me."

He didn't look well at all and spoke in a voice so soft I could barely understand him. It was hard to believe this was the great star with the soaring voice. It turned out this meeting was about more than a new recording contract. For nearly three hours, Roy told me all of what I wrote at the beginning of this chapter and that he was "done being taken advantage of in life." Along with not owning the master recordings for any of his hits or his songs, he told me he needed to get away from Wesley Rose, his manager, label owner, publisher, and trustee of his sons' trust. Rose was also owner of both Acuff-Rose Music, a music publishing firm formed in 1942 by his father, Fred Rose, and the singer Roy Acuff, and Old Hickory Records. Much has been written about these old-school exploiters of talent, who showcased the "snowman" approach of Colonel Tom Parker and his fifty-fifty deal with Elvis Presley. Wesley Rose was no Colonel Parker. But he was trained as an accountant and used that knowledge to ensure he made more than the songwriter signed to him. Rose also went further, actually owning Roy's songs while mismanaging his career and paying him pennies as a songwriter.

My warrior instincts were to attack and break those contracts. However, my first lawyer instinct is always to seek a compromise. I had Roy write a very nice letter to Mr. Wesley Rose advising that he had hired me as his attorney and would appreciate Rose meeting with me. Rose agreed. I called his office in Nashville and set the time and date with the receptionist. When I arrived at the office, I was told that Rose would see me soon. Fifteen minutes later, which I assume was Rose's statement to me indicating he was busy and in control, the receptionist took me back to the dark corner office. Windows weren't a thing back in Nashville.

Rose invited me to sit and proceeded to tell me why I wouldn't be able to help Roy. He said Roy's problems were not his contracts but his life. He said he would give up management on the spot but would never give Roy a share of his songs or even improve his deal.

On that trip to Nashville, my next stop was Roy's house to meet with him and his wife, Barbara, about Rose and their relationship with him now. The Orbisons lived in a beautiful and large home on Old Hickory Lake. It looked kind of like a Swiss chalet and had a beautiful wrought-iron gate similar to the one at Graceland.

I pushed the button and said, "John Mason here to meet Mr. Orbison."

Not a word was said in return, but the gate opened. I drove in and went to the front door, expecting to be met by a housekeeper, but instead the door opened a crack and I saw the face of a woman who looked nothing like the photos I had seen of the beautiful German girl Roy had married just nine years earlier. She opened the door and, as softly as Roy had spoken at our breakfast, said, "Hello, I am Barbara Orbison. Roy is waiting for you."

Upon crossing the threshold, I realized that she was drunk.

Barbara was overweight and pale. She apologized for her condition and said she had not been outside the house for months. "I have agoraphobia and can't go outside," she told me as we sat down with Roy. Over time, I learned that Barbara was seeking help for the agoraphobia and also trying to calm herself with wine and spirits. Oddly, I would never see Roy drink an alcoholic beverage in all the time we worked together. He was truly a teetotaler; water and tea were his go-to drinks.

Notwithstanding Barbara's conditions, the meeting went well, and I was given the go-ahead to take over all of Roy's legal affairs and to let Rose know that he would now have to deal with me directly and not with them. Not surprisingly, the Orbisons didn't have a business manager, as their money was handled by Acuff-Rose.

It didn't take long for my subsequent meetings, calls, and correspondence with Rose to get pretty heated. I realized the only successful way out would be a lawsuit for declaratory relief based on fraud. I told Barbara and Roy what I recommended and that I could bring in a top litigator to take on the giant Acuff-Rose machine. Barbara declined and said, "I have a friend who is a trial lawyer, and I would like to use him."

"Okay," I said reluctantly. The truth was I really didn't know many Tennessee lawyers back then, so Barbara's "friend" got the case. He seemed fine for a while, but then I found he couldn't finish his work. The complaint he had been working on for more than a year grew to hundreds of pages and was generally incomprehensible. I asked around about the guy and finally was told he was in AA with Barbara. It seemed she got well; he didn't.

Working with this lawyer was a nightmare. He might have been a fine lawyer in the past, but he had become irascible and, in my opinion, incompetent, likely from drinking. I would visit him each time I traveled to Nashville during a two-year period. There were papers, documents, and books everywhere, curtains drawn and fluorescent tubes blazing. He would tell me of his brilliant strategies and show me the massive complaint he intended to file. However, he would never give me or Barbara a copy.

She defended him and truly believed he was going to crush Acuff-Rose. He didn't.

He never finished, let alone filed the complaint. I practically begged Barbara to fire him. Roy was distraught, as he still hadn't gotten his songs back and wasn't being paid fairly.

Barbara finally got totally frustrated as well and told her friend he was out. I recommended bringing in the legendary Nashville attorney Aubrey Harwell Jr., and the fireworks soon began.

Barbara and Roy were determined to fight. In turn, Rose vowed to fight to the end. Aubrey's partner was the famous James F. Neal, who had prosecuted the labor leader Jimmy Hoffa and many of the Nixon team involved in the Watergate scandal, along with other high-profile defendants. They were not afraid of Wesley Rose. Then Rose and Roy Acuff ended up selling the company in 1984 to Gaylord Entertainment, who later sold it to Sony/ATV. The fight went on for over a year, but, in my opinion, Rose's tracks could not be covered up and neither Gaylord nor Sony wanted to air his dirty laundry or back up his "creative accounting." They agreed to settle, and Roy got his songs back.

Meanwhile, Barbara's recovery was amazing. She stopped drinking, lost all the extra weight, and took over the business. Getting his songs back was huge for Barbara and Roy, and it afforded them enough money to rerecord all of his hits. Barbara managed the assets and business, and Roy happily hit the road again. Barbara was truly a business genius, and I can't say that about many spouses of my clients. Coincidentally, my wife, Bianca, is also German. She and Barbara had a great relationship and always spoke in German, which I still cannot understand. Once we had resolved the Acuff-Rose litigation and Roy got his songs back, Barbara started Still Working for the Man Music. She bought a former storage building, renovated it into an office, and started signing new songwriters with great success.

I saw Roy a lot over the years. Every time I was in Nashville or out west, we got together, more so after the lawsuit and as friends rather than attorney and client. He had a really cute giggle and enjoyed chatting about everything but music, except for when it came to his awe of other entertainers. By 1986, the business was humming, and the director David Lynch chose to feature

Roy's "In Dreams" in his film *Blue Velvet*. Roy was finally feted for his incredible music and was inducted in 1987 into both the Nashville Songwriters Hall of Fame and the Rock and Roll Hall of Fame.

None other than the legendary Bruce Springsteen introduced Roy at the Rock and Roll Hall of Fame ceremony, proclaiming Roy was the greatest artist ever and that he had worn out his eight-tracks playing Roy's hits over and over. Earlier in his career, Springsteen had famously played tribute to Roy in the lyrics to his classic "Thunder Road," where he painted a picture of Roy "singing for the lonely." Springsteen's public comments that Roy had changed his life truly mattered to Roy.

Roy got back his confidence, his voice, his "look" (now black pants, shoes, shirt, and those glasses). It was great working with Barbara and Roy on contracts for new albums for their publishing company, including *Mystery Girl*, produced by Jeff Lynne of ELO. The single "You Got It," written by Lynne with Tom Petty, was on that record. And in 1988, Roy was asked by Lynne to join a new supergroup to be called the Traveling Wilburys, which would also include Bob Dylan, George Harrison, Petty, and Lynne. Roy was a legend, but being asked to join the Traveling Willburys may have been, in his opinion, the most amazing time of his life.

Barbara really tied it all together when she thought of Roy doing a live concert with an all-star band including Springsteen, Petty, Bonnie Raitt, Elvis Costello, k. d. lang, Jackson Browne, Tom Waits, T Bone Burnett, J. D. Souther, Jennifer Warren, Steven Soles, and Jerry Scheff. The show was performed at the (in)famous Cocoanut Grove, a nightclub at the Ambassador Hotel in Hollywood. Thanks to Barbara, we were able to get funding from a deal with HBO for a special to be filmed at the concert. The show was on September 30, 1987. Bianca and I even flew in from our home in Lake Tahoe to be there. And it was pure magic.

Roy's voice live was crystal clear, pristine, a melancholy sound that invaded your soul, and the "backing band" was ridiculous. There was a special glint in Roy's glasses, by the way—glasses that I'd never seen him remove in the fifteen years we worked together. The show aired on HBO on January 3, 1988. It was a huge success, capturing a magical night when both Barbara and Roy were in great form. She was the ringmaster, running, producing, and directing everything going on, while Roy basked in the glow of the amazing tributes guests paid him.

While they had recorded in 1987, the Wilburys' first single and video, "Handle with Care," was released on October 17, 1988, but Roy would never know what an impact it had. He performed his last concert on December 1, 1988, at the Front Row Theater in Cleveland, Ohio. Five days later, Roy passed away from a heart attack.

In 1987, when Roy was inducted into the Rock and Roll Hall of Fame, Springsteen said, "I'd lay in bed at night with just the lights of my stereo on and I'd hear 'Crying,' 'Love Hurts,' 'Running Scared,' 'Only the Lonely,' and 'It's Over' filling my room."

Bruce went on: "Orbison's voice was unearthly. He had the ability, like all great rock and rollers, to sound like he dropped in from another planet . . . I carry his records with me when I go on tour today, and I'll always remember what he means to me, and what he meant to me when I was young and afraid to love."

It is a beautiful memory that this shy, kind, sweet, and generous man was idolized by the greatest stars in the world. He never claimed credit for that. He just kept writing and singing until his big heart gave out.

"My voice is a gift," Roy said over and over again. "This life is a gift."

7

THE PRINCE OF POP RULES THE WORLD

Don't stop 'til you get enough.
—Michael Jackson

When I was a kid, there were doo-wop groups from New York and then there were five extremely talented young brothers from Gary, Indiana, who joined forces onstage because their father, Joe, a steelworker and former boxer, said so. Joe had a dream; his kids would make it come true.

Michael Jackson, the eighth of Joe's ten children, began performing in the family living room at the tender age of four. The kid loved every part of it. Fast on his feet, he'd glide across those old linoleum floors in a town that was rife with crime, civil unrest, and crushed plans and promises. That didn't matter. Joe wasn't just getting out. His kids were going to turn him into a multimillionaire. To that end, the group he called the Jackson 5 was born.

In 1964, Michael, who was six years old and driven to sing and dance, went to work. The band officially included brothers Jackie, Tito, Marlon, and Jermaine. Rehearsals were long and grueling, while compliments weren't the norm. Michael would remember years later that his father didn't praise his singing ability after that first performance or his magical moves. "He told me I had a big nose," Jackson said. That was just the beginning of Michael's obsession with his looks and planted the seeds for future plastic surgery adventures in the name of finding true "beauty." By the end of his life, the press would print pictures of him and label him a freak.

Back in the day, Joe made all the calls. He would sit at rehearsals with a belt in his hand in case he had to punish any mistakes or misbehavior. Despite the harsh treatment, a singing dynasty was born. Michael Jackson, produced by the musical genius Quincy Jones, went on to become the King of Pop and an icon the world over, selling in excess of a billion records and performing in front of millions of fans. He was a superstar.

But first he was just a kid performing with his brothers.

The Jackson 5 scored their first number one single in 1969 with "I Want You Back." Hit after hit followed, including "I'll Be There," "Never Can Say Goodbye," "Sugar Daddy," and "Dancing Machine." By age eleven, Michael was a sensation, with numerous TV appearances and sold-out shows. By twenty-one, he would release his first solo album, *Off the Wall*, and break away from the brothers who had taught him early dance moves in the living room of their tiny ranch house.

Michael was always the first one to give some of the credit to a mentor who, over his lifetime, would act as his mother, his friend, and some would say his true love. Her name was also well known: Diana Ross. Michael met Diana in 1969 when the Jackson 5 were first signed to Motown. In fact, it was Diana who is credited for discovering the Jackson 5, which is not entirely true (although it made for some great PR). Motown founder Berry Gordy made up that story. The truth is Gladys Knight and the music industry legend Suzanne de Passe discovered the Jackson 5, but that was a far less thrilling story. Berry, who also had a relationship and daughter with Diana, pushed Michael to move in with Diana in 1969. He lived with her for a year until the Jackson family moved from Gary to Encino, California, in 1971. He called her his "girlfriend" and "mamma." No one in the Jackson family seemed to mind, including Katherine Jackson, his biological mother, who wrote in her book that she was fine with her beloved MJ calling Diana "Mamma." Katherine was "fine" with most things.

All I remember personally from those early Michael days is that he had massive talent and a very high voice, and he sang some cute and catchy songs like "ABC." Meanwhile, the rest of the hardworking brothers were under the thumb of their oppressive father. I remember that Jermaine also stuck out because he'd married Gordy's daughter Hazel (although three children later, they called it quits). No one could have predicted that the Jackson 5 would be among the few artists who would leave Motown because the contracts were very company orientated instead of artist focused and the "system" left little room for individual creativity. All the Jackson 5 hits with Motown were written and produced in-house.

The Jackson 5 were definitely a work in progress when they arrived at Gordy's home seeking fame and fortune. They ended up going to the Motown school of performance and songwriting. They didn't even have a separate manager, as Motown kept that type of guidance likewise in-house. Everything was under Gordy's control, which was the way Gordy liked it. Motown was his baby, and his music and vision changed the world.

✦

My involvement with the family didn't begin until about 1976, after Joe broke the boys away from Motown, flying Gordy's coop after his sons achieved sixteen Top 40 singles. They signed with CBS's Epic Records in early 1975, with the notable exception of Jermaine, who was quickly replaced by a very young Randy. New management of the group would still have Joe at the helm with an expanded role. The Jackson patriarch insisted he would now have creative control, which his wife, Katherine, supported as a way of keeping it all in the family.

Joe was also about the money. He wanted to increase his family's take of royalties; they had earned only 2.8 percent with Motown. Joe wanted more—much more—and he had a point. The group was popular. Seats were filled at concerts; records flew off shelves. Epic Records quickly began to negotiate with Joe, and the end result was a lucrative contract and a royalty rate of 20 percent per record. Joe and the boys signed on the dotted line in June 1975.

Motown immediately sued for breach of contract, but at the same time it allowed the group to record for Epic if they changed their name. Motown owned the Jackson 5 name—and it wasn't in a lending mood.

Joe owned the new name: the Jacksons.

✦

In 1976, my friend and client Quincy Jones introduced me to Joe, a man with big plans and a tough guy persona. He also had a particular vision. Joe told me he was basically ready for his young son Randy to break out and become the next big star. Joe actually thought he had that kind of power. Meanwhile, CBS president Walter Yetnikoff and Sony had realized something Joe hadn't:

Michael didn't need the Jacksons, but the Jacksons sure as hell needed Michael.

But Randy Jackson, superstar? I didn't think so. The irony was that Randy has the same name as another Randy Jackson. When you say Randy Jackson, the first thought that comes to mind is the guy from *American Idol*. No relation—*that* Randy Jackson, who is also a talented record producer, is a household name. Randy *from* the Jacksons was always just another Jackson. In other words, he was no Michael.

Joe's pick ultimately couldn't step up, and this was problematic because Jermaine had quit the group and taken with him a substantial following of teenage girls. When Joe came to me in 1976, it was time to renegotiate the Jacksons' contract with CBS and Epic Records. This would lead to their *Destiny* album in 1978, which would mark their first real success in years. I was ready, willing, and able to step in. Yetnikoff and his lieutenants despised me for my independence and Joe liked that fact. He told his sons, "Mason is your new lawyer."

And that was it.

The initial meetings were held at 9200 Sunset Boulevard in my big corner office at the time. I had left Kaplan and was settling into my new digs as my own boss. It wasn't long before the entire Jackson family was in my schedule for half-day meetings that were epic minidramas. Under Joe's system, everyone was required to show up when requested. I'd bring in chairs and put them in a circle in the middle of this gigantic room. The five brothers would sit in the inner circle with their new lawyer (me). But virtually every individual brother also brought with him to the meeting his own personal lawyer, manager, and accountant. These folks sat in a middle circle. There was a third circle behind that one for family members.

Katherine Jackson not only came to meetings but would bring her daughters, Janet, La Toya, and Rebbie. Janet would just wait in the corner bored out of her mind while LaToya would listen attentively. The very back row of this massive gathering also included the muscle: Joe and his thug du jour. Joe liked to hang out with dudes who had criminal backgrounds. Why? He was all about intimidation.

One particular thug at our early meetings was nice enough and not really that threatening, because I'm the son of a butcher who likes to dabble in the martial arts. I didn't sweat the situation. In the end, I had to smile. Turns out the thug also wanted career advice from me, and why not? It was Hollywood, after all.

The first time Joe Jackson came to my office, flanked by a different thug, Joe wasn't happy. He wasn't sure about the Epic Records deal because he wanted his own label, insisting, "It's my family. I'm in charge." The funny thing was that Joe wasn't really acting as the manager to the most important person in the group (Michael) at this point. That job went to a man named Freddy DeMann, a film producer, music executive, and eventual co-founder of Maverick Records. He worked with Michael during three of his most important solo albums, *Off the Wall*, *Thriller*, and *Bad*. During his career, he would not only manage Michael Jackson but also Madonna, Lionel Richie, and Shakira.

Joe felt that he transcended all label jobs. He wasn't Michael's manager, he was way more than that; he was his *father*. I'll never forget the nasty scowl on his face. I don't think the man was actually capable of smiling (and that belief held true, because each time I met with him, he was frowning). Joe tried to establish dominance from the first moment with a death-grip handshake. Though shorter than me, this former steelworker from Indiana was proud of his bone-crunching way of introducing himself. I was ready for him and dug my thumb into the web of his hand, which caused him so much pain that he had to pull back. The thug looked at me in a way that clearly said, *Never do that again to Joe.*

Fine, I thought. *If he doesn't do it, then I won't do it.*

Despite some early jockeying, I was hired, and soon it was time to form those circles of chairs. An assistant ordered sandwiches and sodas, and times were set for the entire group to invade my office. It wasn't long before Michael started coming to every meeting. Shy, thin, and kind with a warm smile, he sat in the inner circle as we began planning for a new Jacksons deal.

He was also in the hot seat. Joe's plan was for all six Jacksons to reunite on what would be the *Destiny* album and then embark on a worldwide tour. Michael was there to listen, flanked by his personal lawyer, David Braun, a super polite type but not as polite as MJ himself.

"Mr. Mason," Michael Jackson told me one day in his high-pitched voice, "I need to have a separate lawyer from my brothers because I want a solo career."

David was a welcome addition. He was a seminal music lawyer, successfully representing the legends Bob Dylan and Neil Diamond. David told me that he didn't really want to be in these meetings, but Michael needed him there. Eventually, there would be another lawyer for Michael, when David took a job as the president of PolyGram Records.

It was David who sent in a young lawyer named John Branca who made me smile. Whenever he opened his briefcase, there would be a tasty-looking sandwich in there in case the meeting ran long. Branca, who represented the Rolling Stones, Carlos

Santana, Aerosmith, and ultimately also the Bee Gees and the Doors, was hired by Michael after David resigned.

Michael and Branca had an up-and-down relationship. He was in; he was out. Michael could be a very difficult guy because he lived in his own artistic world. He didn't want to be bothered by the rest of it. There Michael would be in the inner circle with headphones on his ears during our meeting. He was constantly listening to his Walkman and paying absolutely no attention to what anyone was saying because he couldn't hear them. Instead, music would drift out of the earphones as he intently listened to the beat.

I was trying to run the meeting while the most famous person in the room wasn't hearing one word of it, wasn't paying a second of attention. I would interrupt him and lift one of his earphones to say, "Are you listening, Michael? Hello? Michael?" Or a brother would tap the genius on the shoulder and say, "Michael . . . Michael . . . Mr. Mason is asking you a question."

There were times, however, when he did have something to say. At one meeting, Michael told everyone of his plans to make a groundbreaking solo album. The brothers had a collective attitude of "fine, fine, fine, make your album, as long as you do this tour with us and you're the star of it."

Michael was true to his word. He did work with his brothers again, but at the same time, he had Branca negotiate a solo deal for him for a little album whose tracks he was listening to on that Walkman in my office when he wasn't listening. It was called *Off the Wall*, although later I found out that he had the bones of *Thriller* on those tapes as well.

✦

When I knew him, Michael still looked like the old MJ without all the plastic surgery or skin lightening. It was an interesting time for the family, because though Michael had Branca negotiate a solo deal, Joe was still sure that Randy was the next big star and Michael's time was over.

Meanwhile, the brothers weren't all necessarily on solid ground with Joe. Jermaine and his father weren't seeing eye-to-eye, and he fired Joe as his manager. It didn't matter because Joe said he was at these meetings as the boys' dad and not necessarily their manager. Katherine was there to make sure the boys and their father kept the peace, although she chalked up her presence the supposed lack of babysitters to watch the girls. She was very quiet while Joe was very aggressive in the negotiations. She consoled while he pushed.

In the end, Joe got paid from everything. His hands were in all his sons' pockets. It's no secret that Joe was abusive. He would physically fight his sons if they disagreed with him. In our meetings, he would yell and scream at them, but the grown Jackson men didn't flinch. They were used to the abuse. Desensitized to it. I remember that the brothers would come to each other's defenses in quiet ways. Tito would say, "Come on, Dad, you gotta stop." If Joe was too out of control, Katherine would just sit and glower at him.

✦

Michael was the most fascinating because it was obvious to me that he was very focused on his new music, which didn't involve his brothers. Yet, he had a loyalty to his brothers that was underestimated by the press. He was invested in their success, which is why he agreed to go out on the road with them again.

Thriller was released in 1982, and Michael, who also had a producing deal, had the biggest song of his solo career thus far with the smash "Billie Jean," which dropped on January 2, 1983, as the second single from Jackson's sixth studio album. Michael would tell the press that the lyrics were based on groupies' claims about his older brothers when they were on tour years earlier as the Jackson 5. *Thriller* became the biggest-selling album of all time, with "Billie Jean" and its blend of post-disco, R&B, funk, and dance pop immediately shooting to the number one spot on the *Billboard* chart.

At the height of his fame, with the world trying to stand on their toes like MJ, he kept his word and went on the Victory Tour with his brothers. Fans mostly came to see Michael, figuring that this was his *Thriller* tour. The brothers performed from July to December 1984. The tour grossed $75 million ($232 million in 2024 dollars) and set records as one of the highest-grossing tours of the year. Michael kicked ass on the tour. Without him, it would have never even gotten off the ground.

Negotiating for the Jacksons was one of the most stressful things I ever did in my career. By the time the record and tour contracts were signed, I hadn't been paid a dime from the family in two years. When I asked about money, I heard, "We'll get you later."

Eventually, I got my check. And then I resigned. Life was too short to remain an attorney for the brothers without Michael. The Victory Tour was victorious. There really was nothing more for me to do.

✦

Michael was one of my most famous clients, but he was a very strange person. I don't say that in a negative way at all. Like many iconic artists, he was obsessed with his own persona and his art. At the same time, he didn't want to be bothered by the business of show business. So while he came to every meeting, he would never do what his dad and brothers said. He was his own man, which is also why he was so hugely successful. Michael created his own life, his look, and his music.

People ask me, "Do you think he did those horrible things with kids?"

My answer is that when I knew him, there was absolutely nothing along those lines that was brought to light. Not even a mention or hint. Personally, I don't think it was happening at the time. All I saw was a man in love with his music and who was very close with his mother. Later, he lost all sense of reality and became a punch line.

The man in the mirror mostly remained an enigma.

✦

In 2009, I was living in Reno when I got a call from someone who told me that Michael was in "really bad shape." He was trying to tour again, but he had collapsed onstage during rehearsals. Yet, he was back at it the next day. Michael was Michael. He would not take no for an answer.

He also needed money badly, as he had some bad investments and had put so much money into his music. We talked about how Michael was reportedly using drugs to fall asleep and drugs to wake up.

Elvis lived that life and died because of it. The reason was the same: He needed the cash.

The story remains that Michael was almost bankrupt. He was about to lose his estate, Neverland Ranch. His new doctor ended up giving him too much acute propofol and benzodiazepine to help him sleep, and Michael died on June 25, 2009. The doctor was convicted of manslaughter. Sadly, Michael's last words were: "I can't function if I don't sleep. They'll have to cancel it. And I don't want them to cancel it." He was obsessed with touring again, but it wasn't meant to happen. As for the doctor, he did what too many people do when they work for celebs: Whatever the star wants, the star gets.

I was in Reno when I heard about his passing, and I was not really surprised. It did hurt to see the photos of Michael looking skeletal thin. He never took care of himself other than for the stage. He got fit to do his shows, working his ass off. He was super talented. He was a genius musically. I really got it watching him debut the moonwalk and his signature glove on May 16, 1983, while singing "Billie Jean" on NBC's *Motown 25: Yesterday, Today, Forever* anniversary special. This guy was onto something as he did that backward glide step he learned from street dances. It made your heart race while your jaw dropped. It floored me that all that time in my office those were the songs he was writing and listening to on his Walkman. He never shared the music with any of us, including his brothers. Were the other Jacksons jealous? Probably. Were they in awe of him? Definitely.

There are not any others like him.

Probably never will be.

✦

One last Michael story: I remember the superstar came to his lawyer John Branca's wedding in a military uniform with his pet chimp, Bubbles, in his arms. Bubbles was wearing the exact same military jacket along with a diaper. There was also a handler for the monkey, so Michael could eat his meal and talk to friends. Heads turned to stare at him. Forget the bride. Even at the wedding, Michael was the star.

8

SHAKIRA, SHAKIRA

My brain, I believe, is the most beautiful part of my body.
—Shakira

In the fall of 1999, Emilio Estefan called me. He was super excited and said, "John, I have this great artist here in the studio. I'm also managing her and she needs a lawyer. You need to come to Miami this week to meet her."

Emilio had golden ears and instincts. He also had a golden touch with artists, songwriters, and producers.

"Who is she?" I asked.

The answer was one word: Shakira.

"No last name?" I asked.

"It's Shakira Isabel Mebarak," he said. "But she's already famous as just Shakira."

I had never heard of her. I didn't know her music, either, but did some research and got copies of her then most recent Spanish-language albums, 1995's *Pies Descalzos* and 1998's *Dónde Están los Ladrones?* I was knocked out by her songwriting and stunning voice. I knew enough Spanish to understand the lyrics, especially as I listened to every song over and over again. A week later, I called Emilio to set up a meeting. He did.

The next day, I flew into Miami and went to the address Emilio had given me. It was a beautiful light and airy apartment. I rang the bell and was greeted by both of her parents, William and Nidia, who didn't speak much English. Fortunately, my high school Spanish and the two-week immersion course I had taken in Buenos Aires in 1996 was good enough to communicate with them.

William and Nidia were charming and escorted me into the living room, where Shakira was sitting alone on the couch. She was tiny and fresh-faced, only twenty years old, and had short dyed red hair and wore gray sweats. Her parents left the room, and Shakira and I talked in broken Spanish and broken English for three hours. She had great confidence that she could make the transition from Latin stardom to international superstar. She already had Gloria Estefan as her mentor, songwriting partner, and language coach. Emilio was producing demos, but Shakira knew beyond any doubt that she could produce her own records as she had done so in Colombia.

We agreed to work together that day and spoke virtually every day thereafter until 2002. In fact, she asked me to personally call her each day at 8:00 a.m. Pacific time to make sure she was up and working by noon in Miami.

Emilio was doing a great job as her manager, especially given his long experience with his superstar wife, Gloria. He started lining up concerts for her already rabid Spanish-language fans. By January 2000, she was headlining from San Diego to Santo Domingo.

Bianca and I, often with our four young children, were able to go to several concerts and spend lots of time with "Shaki" (her nickname to all friends and family). She was super kind and gracious with our kids and made them feel like a part of her family.

Each show was an experience that made you feel alive. Her power and movement on stage was mesmerizing. Every outfit, note, and move was calculated to be breathtaking and perfect.

It was time to get Shaki a major deal.

✦

Emilio had a great relationship with Columbia Records (now owned by Sony), and, wisely, Columbia wanted to remain in the Shakira business. Of course, it was complicated.

When Emilio and I were negotiating Shaki's new deal with Columbia Records, we first had to have the approval of Columbia Records, Colombia, which owned her recording contract and had since she was thirteen. They wanted a piece of the English-language international market. Once they approved, we had to negotiate with Bob Summer, the head of CBS Records International. However, the entire deal, once negotiated, had to be approved by CBS chairman Tommy Mottola, a close friend of Emilio's and a huge asset to Gloria.

Tommy, at the time, was married to Mariah Carey. When I called him to confirm all the details, he said, "I'm doing this for Emilio. Shakira is amazing, but she will never be as big as [the Mexican singer] Thalía." We made a twenty-dollar bet, and you can guess who won! By the way, Tommy is now married to Thalía.

Plans were set for the new album, which became *Laundry Service* and would feature the single "Whenever, Wherever," which would become Shakira's first huge international English-language hit.

Getting that contract done was a huge undertaking. Emilio and I wanted more from Columbia than even Gloria had, including higher royalties, bigger advances, and a massive promotion and marketing fund. For me, it meant daily calls with Summer, who had to get approval of everything from Mottola. I, of course, reported daily to Emilio and separately to Shakira, who is a perfectionist in everything she does. No matter what I was able to secure, her first question was always "Can we do better?"

When I had finally negotiated the deal and contract far enough to recommend it to Shaki, she asked me to come to Miami to go through it with her. I was again greeted by her lovely parents and found Shaki at the dining room table with the Columbia contract spread out in front of her. She had wanted to have it as early as possible to read every word. She had to get what she wanted or she wouldn't do it.

Ten hours later, we had been through every line of every page and took a break for dinner. I remember those long days into nights, sitting together on the sofa or at her table poring over long documents. She didn't just go through the lines and words, but would ask, "What does that mean? Why is it there? Can we change it?" The questions were detailed and well-thought-out. She needed to know what it all meant, which was admirable. It made her an artist and a businesswoman.

Those ten-hour meetings continued for every contract I worked on with Shakira. She is brilliant and in control on the stage, in the studio, and with her advisers. Every step of the way, it was her way.

✦

We all knew that Shakira needed a full-time manager, and I recommended to Emilio and Shakira that we ask Freddy DeMann, who had already retired after managing Madonna, Michael

Jackson, and Lionel Richie, if he would get back in the game. She truly needed someone who had no other clients but all the experience of working with superstars. Emilio agreed that Freddy was a great choice.

The only problem was Freddy told me many times that he would never be a manager again. Why would he after working with those talents? It's a thankless job. If you don't believe me, just watch him with Madonna in the *Madonna: Truth or Dare* documentary. Plus, he no longer needed the money.

I still called him.

"Freddy," I said, "as your friend, I am begging you to go to Miami to meet one of the greatest artists on the planet. She is Colombian and has only sung and written in Spanish, but when you meet her and listen to her music, you will thank me for the introduction."

"I will never manage anyone again, John," he reminded me.

Yet, he agreed to do me the favor of going to see her. Frankly, this was quite a face-saver for me, since I had raved to Shakira about Freddy and convinced her to let him come.

Freddy lived in Los Angeles, and on the morning of the meeting in Miami, he called me from LAX.

"I'm sorry, John. I was thinking of a different Latina," he said. (It was Thalía.) "I was listening to Shakira on the way to the airport. I don't understand any of the lyrics and want to pass."

I was dumbfounded. "Freddy, you can't do that to me. You promised, and if you don't go, I may get fired. I promise you won't be disappointed."

I was ready to burst with pride when Freddy called me from Miami the next day to say he had spent ten hours with Shakira (pretty normal for her) and was ready to get on board. He had his lawyer send me the proposed management contract the next day. I was in Miami for another ten-hour meeting with Shakira to explain it. Hey, I'm not complaining. Every meeting with Shaki was special, and I wish every artist had an interest in what I do.

Freddy also had a great relationship with CBS Records from his management of Michael Jackson. Mine was excellent as well, especially from the great success we had with Gloria Estefan. Off we went to New York to close a new deal, one of the greatest of my career, followed by another ten-hour meeting with Shakira to explain it. With his past management of Madonna and Michael, Freddy knew where to go for the sponsorships, tour promotion, merchandise deals, and product endorsements. We made a great team.

Part of that teamwork included finding the right tour sponsor. Both Freddy and Emilio had great relationships with Pepsi (in fact, it was Freddy who made Michael Jackson's deal for the commercial where his hair famously caught fire). In March 2001, we all met (including Shakira) with the Pepsi execs and put together Shakira's first major tour sponsorship, which was a major win.

Everything was now set.

Laundry Service was released in November 2001, and the tour started a year later. She called it the Tour of the Mongoose. The album has sold more than 13 million copies worldwide. We did it! The team, especially the captain, came through. Shakira's albums were so big, they put her on the cover of *Rolling Stone*.

I think Freddy's relationship with his only client actually diminished my role in her life. After Pepsi signed on to sponsor her tour, we went to Reebok. Freddy and Shakira, however, wanted more than Reebok ever offered. When Freddy brought the lawyer for Reebok to her house to discuss the company's tour sponsorship proposal, her then "fiancée," Antonio de la Rúa, saw it as the opportunity to replace me with someone of his own choice.

I remember when Shakira met Antonio, whose father had briefly been president of Argentina. In fact, I was there backstage at her huge outdoor concert in Buenos Aires on May 12, 2000. Antonio was a handsome, charming young lawyer with all the bells and whistles of the son of a president. Soon, he moved to Miami and in with Shakira. It wasn't long before he started attending meetings to learn about the entertainment business and help Shakira understand her contracts even better. Since he was a lawyer, even though he had zero experience, he became convinced, and swayed Shakira, that he should be in charge of her legal affairs. He didn't have the audacity to go after Freddy or Emilio.

At some point, they became engaged, although every time I saw Shakira in public, she put the ring on her other hand with the diamond facing her palm. At the time, I was also involved with the negotiations of her personal life, including her engagement to Antonio. Her parents wanted to know about prenups and what they meant. Again, her parents were very close and involved.

"The drafting of a prenup would make it more official and far more difficult for her to walk away," I advised them. In the end: No prenup.

I don't think she ever planned to marry him. In 2011, Shakira announced on her website that after eleven years together, she and Antonio were splitting up. Afterward, claiming he managed her business and career interests, he filed a lawsuit against her for

$250 million. It was dismissed by a Los Angeles Superior Court in August 2013. Shakira would go on to have a relationship with the Spanish football player Gerard Piqué, the father of her sons, Milan and Sasha. They would eventually separate after eleven years together as well.

Somehow, during the negotiation of the Reebok deal, I was replaced by Reebok's own outside counsel. That made no sense to me, as no one should hire the other side's attorney to represent them both. Ultimately, the attorney and Antonio were pushed out of Shakira's life as well.

✦

Shakira creates her own universe. "I'm a perfectionist in recovery," she has said. "I'm trying to deal with that monster inside of me that wants to do everything right. Or better than right."

She was just as exacting when it came to the work. Each track on every album had to be perfect; each dance move was cutting-edge and executed beyond expectations. Her *El Dorado* special was shot over a long period of time. You can see her input, which was basically Shakira working on moves with the dancers and mixing the sound until she was ultimately happy with the end results.

She was just as detailed about every aspect of her life, including money. Shaki has always made big money but could be extremely cheap. She wanted the top people but wasn't willing to pay top price. She never wanted to pay top dollar for anything and was always renegotiating. Freddy may have been the only person who got what he asked for, but she wore him out as well.

She once told me her desire to pay the least was because she wanted to have more than $100 million on hand in the bank at all times. Her family was treated generously while she skimped in other areas. She bought a beautiful home in the Bahamas but not a superstar mansion. She loved any agreement with corporate write-offs. Her tax plans were exacting, too. Perhaps too much so, at least in the eyes of the Spanish government.

Her only weakness was clothes. One of her contracts stipulated that she would have thirty-five new outfits every three months because Shakira didn't want to wear the same thing twice on her tour—and she didn't.

Shakira remains a superstar with no signs of stopping. I loved watching her halftime performance with Jennifer Lopez at Super Bowl LIV in 2020 in front of 50 million people. As a writer, artist, producer, and director, she's at the top of her game as someone who can package herself in all departments. Even with two young children, Shakira continues to record and tour, although there are fewer records now and some complications in her life.

She remains generous to her family and her charities, where she gives away a lot of her money—I know she has given over $100 million to charity. The Pies Descalzos Foundation, which she dreamed up as a little girl, was founded in Colombia during the late '90s when Shakira was only eighteen. It continues to provide shoes for kids who need them throughout the world as well as strives to improve the education, nutrition, and health of the most vulnerable children.

By the way, the tours remain incredible, with Shakira selling out fifty-thousand-seat venues and arenas in Latin America's biggest soccer stadiums. She can sell out seventy- to eighty-thousand-seaters, too. She has the confidence and is so prepared for each show that there is little possibility for a mistake. She remains as driven and talented as the day I met her.

All she has to do is go out there and be Shakira. She doesn't have to think about it but just do it. She walks out onstage and delivers all the thrills. Most of all, she knows who she is, what she wants, and what she is capable of in life and in her career.

Genius.

9

THE LAST DANCE (DONNA SUMMER)

God had to create disco music so that I could be born and be successful.
—Donna Summer

C asablanca Records founder Neil Bogart did not create Donna Summer. Donna Adrian Gaines did. She grew up in Boston, the daughter of a butcher and a teacher who raised her and her six siblings. Except for the last part, we had so much in common.

Her father cut and sold meat. Mine did the same. Both of us got our first taste of performing young. I had my teenage band; she had the big voice and practiced using it at church from the age of ten. We were both destined for bigger things, which led us to work together for so many years.

We also had that work ethic in our DNA. Donna was the go-go-go type who looked only forward. Case in point: Donna performed in school musicals, but she didn't sing at graduation because she wasn't there. She was too busy working in New York, singing with a blues rock band, and didn't have time to get a cap and gown. As the song goes, she worked hard for the money.

Her work life actually began in the theater. A young Donna had a role in Broadway's latest hit, the counterculture musical

Hair. Donna wasn't asked to perform with the New York cast, but she helped bring the show to Munich after her parents reluctantly said yes. Musicals led to releasing her first album. Donna was "discovered" in Germany by the amazing producer and writer Giorgio Moroder—again, not Neil Bogart. Her first album was released in 1974 only in the Netherlands by Groovy Records. An error in printing the cover turned "Donna Sommer" into "Donna Summer" (she had married the Austrian actor Helmuth Sommer in 1973).

She never corrected it.

The following year, lightning struck, and "Love to Love You Baby" became a giant success all over the world. Donna quickly became the Queen of Disco, although her voice and talent overcame that label and brought her hit after hit for another fifteen-plus years.

✦

I became Donna's attorney just after she moved back to the United States in 1976, having been introduced and recommended by then chairman of the William Morris Agency (WMA), Norman Brokaw. Her young manager, Susan Munao, had been an exec at Casablanca and was one of the first female personal managers ever. They were a great pair, with Susan tackling the world and speaking for Donna in the same voice. However, Donna, as well as being talented, was incredibly brilliant, and when it came to business and legal matters, she was always directly involved.

Norman was a true old-school agent: black suit, white shirt, and tie every day. In fact, that was required dress for men at WMA. (There were so few female agents that they didn't have a dress code.) He had started, like all WMA agents back then, in the famous mailroom. Norman was promoted to Marilyn Monroe's driver and then talent agent, representing Monroe, Bill Cosby, Mark Spitz, Warren Beatty, Clint Eastwood, Gerald Ford, and many more, including a new singing talent named Donna Summer. He turned all that into a powerhouse career and the highest title at the legendary agency, becoming the president, chief executive officer, and chairman of WMA.

Norman's policy was to have annual client meetings where his clients sat at the head of the big table behind a name plaque proclaiming "Chairman of the Board." My first meeting with Donna and Susan was on one of those occasions. Donna truly was the chairman of the board. She had the brains, the talent, and the vision. Norman had told Donna and Susan that the singer would need the top entertainment lawyer in LA and recommended only me.

"Don't ever forget, Donna," he told her during one of our group meetings. "You're the chairman of the board."

Once, he gave her an actual gavel that was engraved with "Chairman of the Board." The rest of us were there to help and advise her as she became a superstar to rival all the great voices of the past.

When it came to Donna's voice, you would never know from her singing, but she had a strong Boston accent and a wicked sense of humor. Despite her "sexy" hits and giant fame, Donna was always first a wife and a mom. Her husband, Bruce Sudano, and her three daughters always meant more to her than her career. She was able to manage her relationships with other stars and her label, but she relied on her manager and close friend, Susan Munao, to take care of business.

✦

Yes, Donna had more than a voice in common with other divas of the day. But she never forgot that she was ultimately in charge.

It was clear Neil Bogart and Casablanca Records played a huge role in her success and launched her career in North America in 1975 with the *Love to Love You Baby* album and its many hit singles. However, Donna was already a huge sensation in Europe before he even heard her. Once he did, he opened Casablanca's very limited checkbook and broke her records wide open.

At the beginning of my relationship with Neil and Casablanca, everyone was friendly and supportive, but when it came time for me to demand both improved deal points and significantly large royalties, Neil was adamantly opposed and, in my opinion, thought he and his promotion and marketing teams were more important than the artist. His ego had no bounds. Donna had also become Neil's cash cow, and he didn't want to share the wealth.

We were on a collision course.

Donna's stardom was underestimated during those early years. The story goes that Neil played the unreleased "Love to Love You Baby" single at one of his super-extravagant industry parties, and the crowd loved it so much that they asked him to play it again and again all night long. Neil even asked Donna to do an extended seventeen-minute version, which proved to be a big hit in clubs and discos, while the shorter version received wide radio play. If you went to a club in those days, you needed to have stamina, because seventeen minutes on the dance floor was cardio before people even talked about cardio.

The record went platinum and sold over a million copies. You couldn't beat the controversy, either. Donna emitted several sexy moans on the album and breathy seconds, which some stations found objectionable and overly sexual, verging on pornographic. You couldn't buy that kind of PR.

By 1977, "I Feel Love," off her fifth album, *I Remember Yesterday*, reached number six on the Hot 100 charts and number one in the UK. It later went gold, while the album went platinum in the United States. That same year her double album *Once Upon a Time* also hit gold.

Donna's star continued to rise. By 1978, her song "Last Dance" reached number three, and Donna won her first Grammy Award for Best Female R&B Vocal Performance. It wasn't long after before her Jimmy Webb–penned ballad, "MacArthur Park," became her first number one hit single on the Hot 100 chart, topping the charts for three weeks. Donna would go on to become the first female artist of the modern rock era to have the number one single on the Hot 100 and the number one album on the Billboard 200 simultaneously. By 1979, there were five big hits: "Hot Stuff," "Bad Girls," "Heaven Knows," "Dim All the Lights," and "No More Tears (Enough Is Enough)."

As her star rose and Donna Summer became a household name, her old deal with Neil became an issue.

I remember driving over to Casablanca on Sunset Boulevard one day to talk about a new deal for Donna, who wasn't being paid what she was worth. Not even close. From Donna and Susan's point of view, we could easily make a new deal with Neil. He was their "friend." From my point of view that day, he was imploding. I'd watched him fall off his chair after snorting something, and there were rumors that he was "inappropriate" with secretaries. I despised this stereotypical 1970s lifestyle, but we had a contract renewal to discuss.

Casablanca did a lot in terms of launching Donna's career, and she was the loyal type. Donna didn't want to believe that after all the success they'd had together that Neil wouldn't pay her fairly.

The mood was chilly when we went into negotiations.

Neil made it clear that he refused to negotiate almost anything favorable to Donna. "She would be nothing without me," he said to me over and over again. "I will never let her leave the label, no matter what."

Before me in those meetings was an erratic and inconsistent man. I looked into his eyes and knew he must have been taking drugs. Cocaine was extremely prevalent back then, especially in the music business, and used by artists and executives.

I had been privy to other horror stories of working under Neil at Casablanca. I didn't trust him and told Donna so. One time, during a meeting in his office on Sunset, he actually took out a paper with white powder on it and snorted it through a straw. As her attorney, I had to tell Donna what I had observed as well as Neil's refusal to negotiate in her favor. She told me she wanted "off the label." I told Neil, but he refused despite her long list of grievances.

Her gripes: Casablanca wanted her to record only disco songs. Donna was also upset with Neil over the early release of her duet with Barbra Streisand called "No More Tears (Enough Is Enough)." Barbra and Donna had mutually decided they would release the single at the same time on their separate labels. Casablanca got its record out early and before her previous single, "Dim All the Lights," had peaked. At one point, the surprise early release of "Enough Is Enough" battled indirectly with "Dim All the Lights." Donna beat out herself: "Enough" was number one; "Dim" was number two. No one knew how it got out early, which didn't sit well with Donna, who had written "Dim." It was the first song she'd written alone, and she hadn't wanted anything interrupting the song's rise and stay at the top of the charts.

Despite this glitch, working with Barbra Streisand was one of the highlights of Donna's life. The press always likes to turn two women working together into rivals, but the "claws" never came out. It was a lovefest instead. Donna was thrilled to work with the legend and vice versa. They wanted the deal to be fair so everyone felt good about it, and the one we cut with Barbra's manager, Martin "Marty" Erlichman, couldn't have been more perfect: the artists were equal in the deal as well as the record's royalties.

Barbra was already a music legend, but she was determined that Donna feel good about the project. She was very conscious about how things were recorded and ensured everything in the studio was set up properly so she and Donna could sing their collective hearts out. Both had soaring voices that complemented each other beautifully. Neither outpowered the other, which was a conscious choice by each singer. Barbra was very sweet to Donna, who always said, "We had a great time and a great relationship." There were sessions together and long dinners, plus conversations that would never be repeated.

The fact that they sang the song together in the studio, which most of the time isn't the case, was a miracle. Barbra would insist on doing that with Sinatra for his *Duets* album—and was the only singer granted that wish.

Donna raved about the experience. She finished up the project knowing she wasn't just a Streisand fan, but Barbra was also a Donna fan.

✦

Things didn't always go so smoothly.

I was forced to tell Neil that if he didn't let her go, regardless of our willingness to give him a piece of future income, I would have to recommend to Donna that she file an action to terminate her recording agreement. Even though he was in the process of selling Casablanca to PolyGram, he refused to even negotiate. I knew instinctively that Donna needed to get out and pronto. But Neil wouldn't make that deal, so it would be on me to work on him as I fought her out of her contract.

I had worked many cases with a lawyer named Don Engel, who moved from New York to LA in 1973. He knew the lawyer Harold Lipton (actress Peggy Lipton's father), and he introduced us. Don was a great New York litigator, and his wife, Judy, was his partner. I used them when I represented Olivia Newton-John against Universal and later on with the rocker Sammy Hagar. Don also joined the Donna Summer contract project with just one goal: Free Donna.

It wasn't easy because Neil wanted to keep his big star and he had an out-of-control ego. We had meetings that led to us being mortal enemies. Donna just rode it out, telling me, "I'm just the singer. You're the lawyer."

In 1980, I recommended to Donna that she file an action for declaratory relief, asking a court to invalidate the contract due to fraud and undue influence based on Casablanca's long-term control, including the years of "management" by Neil's wife, Joyce, who was on both sides of the deals and contracts. We also filed for damages based on what I saw and believed to be substantial royalty accounting underpayments.

PolyGram took over Casablanca, and Neil's role in the litigation was marginalized. Clearly, he was instructed to get out and be quiet if he wanted to stay on with Casablanca. From that point on, I would deal only with attorneys for PolyGram. We succeeded in having the contract declared unenforceable based upon a "key man" clause requiring Neil's day-to-day control of the company. However, in order to get out of the litigation and to move on with her career and life, Donna agreed that if Casablanca would release her, she would give it one future and final album.

When Donna was free of the Casablanca chokehold, I went out to find her the best deal ever made at one of the best labels she could work with. One of my first calls was to the legendary Walter Yetnikoff, chairman of CBS Records. He agreed to meet with me and even had a car pick me up at JFK Airport in New York. I needed to stop for a meeting with Donna's business manager, David Gotterer, on the way from the airport. His office was in the Warner Communications office building, where we would discuss my proposal. The car waited, then took me over to CBS.

When the elevator door opened on the executive floor, I was met by a screaming Dick Asher, head of CBS International, who accused me of using their car to first meet with Atlantic Records (a division of Warner Communications). I didn't, but Asher would not listen and asked me to leave. I did, but then called Walter to reset the meeting. He asked me to come by the next day. I did, but I walked this time.

When I finally was sitting across from Walter, he said, "How do I know you actually represent Donna Summer? Put her on the phone." I did, but when she answered, he said, "How do I know you are really Donna Summer? Sing me 'Love to Love You.'"

She did, but we made no progress on the deal. Fortunately (or not), David Geffen had left Warner Communications and started his Geffen Records label. His first signings were John Lennon and Elton John. He wanted Donna and didn't make her sing for him. We made an amazing deal for Donna, but pursuant to our settlement agreement with PolyGram, which had bought Casablanca, Donna could make one album for Geffen, but the next had to be for Casablanca. The Geffen album, called *The Wanderer*, was not a big success. Her next album, which went to Casablanca, was *She Works Hard for the Money*, and it was huge.

In 1982, she recorded her first album without Giorgio Moroder and the only one with the brilliant Quincy Jones at the helm. It was not successful. Donna told me she and Q just didn't hit it off creatively in the studio and that he wanted her to sound "more black."

Later, Donna would have a huge falling out with David over her religious belief that homosexuality was a sin. She moved on, with David's blessings, to Atlantic Records, a part of the Warner group of labels.

Still, her career remained on fire. Network specials followed in the early '80s on ABC. She also became pregnant with her daughter Brooklyn at the time and slowed down her pace.

Her life had come full circle.

From that point on, she would hit the studio and then the road. With Susan, we were like brother and sisters, a traveling family.

I'll never forget Donna playing Las Vegas. We planned it far ahead, but when she sang "Bad Girls," I walked onto the stage in front of a packed audience playing a cop in full uniform. Don Engel was the flasher, and Susan was the hooker.

Oh God, she loved it!

So did I.

I also loved watching her write songs. She based them on pictures. She'd look at a photo or painting and create a story and then the song. She wrote a lot of her music in the studio as a melody was being played.

Donna was the best. She cared so much for her people and loved helping anyone in need. Donna was the definition of a generous spirit. She was a giver without a doubt because she was so grateful for her amazing life.

10

COUNTRY QUEEN (REBA MCENTIRE)

To succeed in life, you need three things: a wishbone,
a backbone and a funny bone.
—Reba McEntire

Reba McEntire was born in McAlester, Oklahoma, and raised on a ranch in Chockie. Her dad was a rodeo champion, and Reba was a barrel racer. She remembers singing in public for the first time when she was four years old. She told me that she just wanted to sing for the cowboys.

"One of them gave me a nickel, which was the first time I was paid for singing a song," she recalled. "I thought, 'This is a pretty good thing.'"

It turned out to be a pretty good thing for me, too! Reba is a massive talent and a spitfire to be sure, but I've known a different Reba: a determined woman with backbone who knows what she wants and then goes out to get it. The proof is in the fact that she would come to my office fifty times to talk, arriving like a storm front and disagreeing with me with gusto forty-nine of those visits, until that moment where she proclaimed in that country-tinged tone, "Okay, I see it." That's pure Reba.

Reba takes stardom and her career mega seriously, partly because she has been at it forever. The other part is a great heart and a drive that's in her DNA. Most of all, though, it's a work ethic that won't quit; she's the ultimate hard worker. I used to have an office in Reba's building. She came in every single day she wasn't on tour except for Sundays, which was for church and family. She was always working, whether it was answering fan mail or making sketches for her clothing line or listening to potential new songs.

It's no wonder that her rule over the country music charts hasn't ended.

✦

I met Reba through my friend and client Jimmy Bowen, the guy who hired me when he was president of MGM back in 1972. By 1986, Bowen had moved on to be president of MCA Nashville. He produced Reba, who was looking for new representation and a new MCA deal. Bowen told Reba to talk to me, and she was game. In fact, Reba was a happy woman. She had just gotten engaged, in the most secret way, to her manager and former steel guitar player Narvel Blackstock, and her career was launching toward the stratosphere.

Jump to August 1, 1988.

Bianca and I had been married only a few months and were on our first trip together to Nashville. Bowen had formally recommended that Reba and Narvel meet with me to talk about replacing her outgoing manager and lawyer. It was a great meeting in their brand-new offices in what looked to have been an old exhibition hall on the Nashville fairgrounds, soon to become the home of Starstruck Entertainment.

Great meeting! I was hired on the spot.

Bianca and Reba started a bond that continues to this day. However, when Bowen's boss at the time (Irving Azoff) heard the news, he called Narvel to tell him the only way to get the best deal for Reba with MCA was to hire his handpicked attorney, John Branca. Reba called me to break the news. That's who she is as a person. Reba is never afraid to make a decision, always accepting responsibility for it. Of course I was disappointed, but I kept her and Narvel's phone numbers and moved on. So did they.

From that August to March 1991, Reba cemented her status as a country icon, a one-name wonder who would in her career sell more than 75 million records worldwide with over a hundred singles on the Billboard Hot Country Songs chart, twenty-five of which would climb to the number one spot. I was sure I "missed the boat" personally as well as professionally.

Her life and career seemed perfect. Reba and Narvel said their "I do's" on a private boat in Lake Tahoe, and together it was decided that he would manage Reba's career and business through Starstruck Entertainment. The family was about to expand. Reba gave birth to their son, Shelby Steven McEntire Blackstock, in February 1990.

A year later, the bottom dropped out. On March 16, 1991, after a concert in San Diego, California, Reba's band flew ahead of her, Narvel, and her stylist Sandi Spika. The plane carrying them crashed within minutes of taking off. Seven members of Reba's band and her tour manager were killed.

I don't think she will ever get over the tragedy. In fact, she dedicated her next album, *For My Broken Heart*, to the friends she lost. The album reached number one on the Billboard Top Country Albums chart and is reported to have sold more than 4 million copies.

Bianca and I heard the terrible news on television that night, and I felt compelled to call her the next morning to see if I could help in any way. She called me back later that day.

"You don't know how much that call meant to me," she said. "My own lawyer didn't call or write me or Narvel."

Later that day, Narvel called to let me know they were changing lawyers.

It was the second start to an amazing and decades-long relationship. We were so close that Reba even shot an album cover on our deck in Lake Tahoe, plus sent her son, Shelby, to stay with us and flew us to shows on her private jet more than a dozen times.

Friendship, loyalty, and honesty meant and still means everything to Reba. She arrives by herself with no posse to virtually every special event a friend invites her to attend. Reba and Narvel not only accepted our request to become godparents to our daughter Milana, but then they flew on their jet at their own expense to Lake Tahoe for her First Communion.

Can you imagine the double and triple takes from parishioners at Our Lady of Tahoe when the red hair flashed by and the Queen of Country sat in a pew?

✦

Often, I think it looks like success comes easy, as if talent is always enough. In my case, luck (being in the right place at the right time) played a big part (*crazy lucky*). But for Reba, enormous talent, hard work, and strategy tipped the scale in favor of superstardom. She just didn't stop. Reba came to the office by day for business, then listened to songs and spoke with producers every night. My clients Jimmy Bowen and Tony Brown produced virtually all Reba's hits, and both told me how many hundreds of songs they carefully chose to submit to Reba to get to the final dozen that would make it onto the album.

Recordings were generally done in the evening, after Reba had finished her "normal" day, and continued until around midnight. She used her own band, rather than just session players, and coproduced every track, spending as much time behind the console as in the studio. The results? Hit after hit after hit, including "Whoever's in New England," "Fancy," "Does He Love You," "I'm a Survivor," "Turn On the Radio," "Can't Even Get the Blues," and more. No wonder she couldn't get the blues. Even her cover of Vicki Lawrence's classic ballad "The Night the Lights Went Out in Georgia" raced up the charts.

All of a sudden, Reba was everywhere—and it couldn't have happened to a nicer person. But, I can tell you, she earned it as well! Reba can outwork me to this day!

Between 1991 and 2005, Reba reached basically every career goal possible, including performing at the Academy Awards, starring in two Broadway plays (*Annie Get Your Gun* and *South Pacific*) and her successful television series, *Reba*, and producing the Reba clothing line. Despite being busy, she always had time to be a mom to Shelby and her stepchildren, plus she was such a loyal friend.

In 1993, Reba found the song "Does He Love You," and rather than ask another superstar to sing it with her, she asked her friend and backup singer Linda Davis to co-sing the leads. Another number one single was launched.

Reba took it all in stride and remained amazing. Reba has always been Reba, on and off stage. (In 2005, she launched her Reba clothing line with Dillard's department store. Today, a lot of artists do their own line, but back then it was considered risky and "selling out." Reba, already busier than ever and making enough money to be comfortable, successfully launched the line into the hearts and souls of her fans. I guess I didn't realize growing up that fashion is seasonal and that new lines have to be designed, developed, and marketed quarterly. Reba did. Every product every season had to be submitted to and approved by her personally. However, that was just the creative side. For me, and ultimately Reba, who was sued by her agent/manager for commissions, the fashion industry was just basically risky and too time consuming.)

Meanwhile, back in 1991, Narvel and Reba decided to buy a property on Nashville's Music Row for their office and studios. As always, everything would be done "first class!" In 1997, we made a new deal with MCA, and the Starstruck building and studios were built. Both are still state-of-the-art. I had an office there until 2022, when Jay DeMarcus's Red Street Records made an offer Narvel couldn't refuse and took over all available space. Happily, everyone won! Reba, Narvel, and MCA continued their long run of success. That is until 2009, when the 1997 contract ended and the hottest label in Nashville, Big Machine, gave Reba the opportunity to reunite with Scott Borchetta, the former head of promotion at MCA for virtually all of Reba's hits. Strangely, her records there just never caught fire. I hear Reba is back at Universal (MCA) now.

✦

On a personal note, Reba and I remained close friends. She was the most gracious dinner guest at our homes in Beverly Hills and Nashville. I watched as Narvel's son Brandon Blackstock went on to become a talent manager. He not only managed Kelly Clarkson, who became famous on *American Idol*, but married her. Kelly and Brandon moved to LA to promote *The Voice* in the early days—and more recently went through a nasty divorce that made tabloid headlines.

They weren't the only ones, historically speaking, in the family to call it quits.

Reba's life was jolted in August 2015 when she learned from her husband of twenty-six years that he wanted a divorce. I remember walking into their building that day and hearing the news from their company president, who came downstairs to tell me. My first questions: "What does Reba think? And what happens next?"

"I don't want to get divorced," Reba told me when everything hit the skids in her personal life. "But he's been cheating on me."

It was shocking to me. I hadn't seen divorce on the horizon, but couples have a way of falling off cliffs, especially when they're rich, famous, and being pulled in a million directions. Being married to any celebrity is tough going. Almost everywhere you go, it becomes about the fame, and the public feels as if they have the right to pounce. Privacy is only behind locked gates and doors—and sometimes those measures don't even work. The spouse who isn't famous often feels as if they have to be "on" all the time.

In the end, Narvel found someone else who didn't require him to be the ultimate celebrity accessory. Instead of his fancy duds, he goes around now in T-shirts and jeans.

I've never seen him so relaxed.

✦

The first days with solo Reba were chaos, with issues ranging from navigating their continued management relationship to where she would have an office. The tension was suffocating. I had never seen Reba so out of sorts, which was natural given the circumstances but still jarring.

As their lawyer, I met with them separately several times during the divorce to work things out and sort out the rest. Fortunately, Shelby was already an adult. There were a lot of assets. It wasn't just money but wonderful personal items that were important to both, including precious art, furniture, wine, and cars. Of course, these are just things, and when the people are reasonable, the things fall where they may in these high-profile divorces. There wasn't any fighting or serious disputes as these two parted. The three of us agreed to make it amicable, which is how I always try to handle my clients' divorces. Breaking up is stressful enough; you don't need any extra heartache.

By the way, you won't find any court papers on their split. I figured out how to do that in order to protect their privacy.

"I'm not sure what I'm going to do now," Reba told me when it was over.

Reba rebounded with a vengeance, including a sold-out Vegas residency with Brooks and Dunn. She decided to manage herself and moved to set up her own management company while also becoming financially independent. She also shook up her team and hired a new business manager and a nearly all-female staff. Four months later, after thirty years together, I was out. My job went to an attorney in the new business manager's camp in Atlanta.

As for Reba, she seems happy since the split. She realized that their collective lives were not their own. It's a burden to live in the ever-changing, high-pressure fast lane of the music business. The upshot is they have an amazing son who is a race car driver.

Reba is a mom to many, which reflects her warm, caring core. We talk every once in a while. I smiled when she told me she was dating two different guys but would never be in a situation "where any man tells me what to do."

"I feel free," she told me.

I think that's a great ending . . . or new beginning.

11

COUNTRY KING (KENNY ROGERS)

*If the president of my label doesn't want me to hire you,
I am positive you will be great for me.*
—Kenny Rogers

I met Kenny Rogers by chance back in 1972, when he was still in the soon-to-break-up group the First Edition, but after they'd changed their name to Kenny Rogers and the First Edition. This evolution was for their hit "Ruby, Don't Take Your Love to Town," where his vocals made it a smash. They also made the name change to have the chance to have two records on the radio at the same time by using two different names. Their records were produced by my friend and client Jimmy Bowen, who introduced us when Kenny dropped in. The singer wasn't there to "see what condition my condition was in," which was also produced by Bowen, but for a creative meeting on what the future might hold for Kenny as a solo artist, whose group was about to hit the skids; his career was at a crossroads.

Immediately, Kenny struck me as a gentle, kind, and humble man who was not at all awed by his own success. He was practical and realistic, too. He had been in a couple of bands in the past without success, so he appreciated the new hits, knowing they might not happen again.

Early guitar lesson with Duke Snyder.

First "glam" photo in "Nudie's" shirt handmade by Manuel Cuevas.
Circa 1958.

My group The Vulcanes.

Me on the lobby card for the film *I'll Take Sweden* where I got to play and act with my friend Frankie Avalon.

"Caught with our pants down." First PR photo for my lawfirm, Garey, Mason and Sloane.

With Eddie Rabbitt after Houston Livestock and Rodeo show in the Astrodome
(about 90,000 fans went crazy) .

On stage with Donna Summer in Las Vegas. Circa 1982.

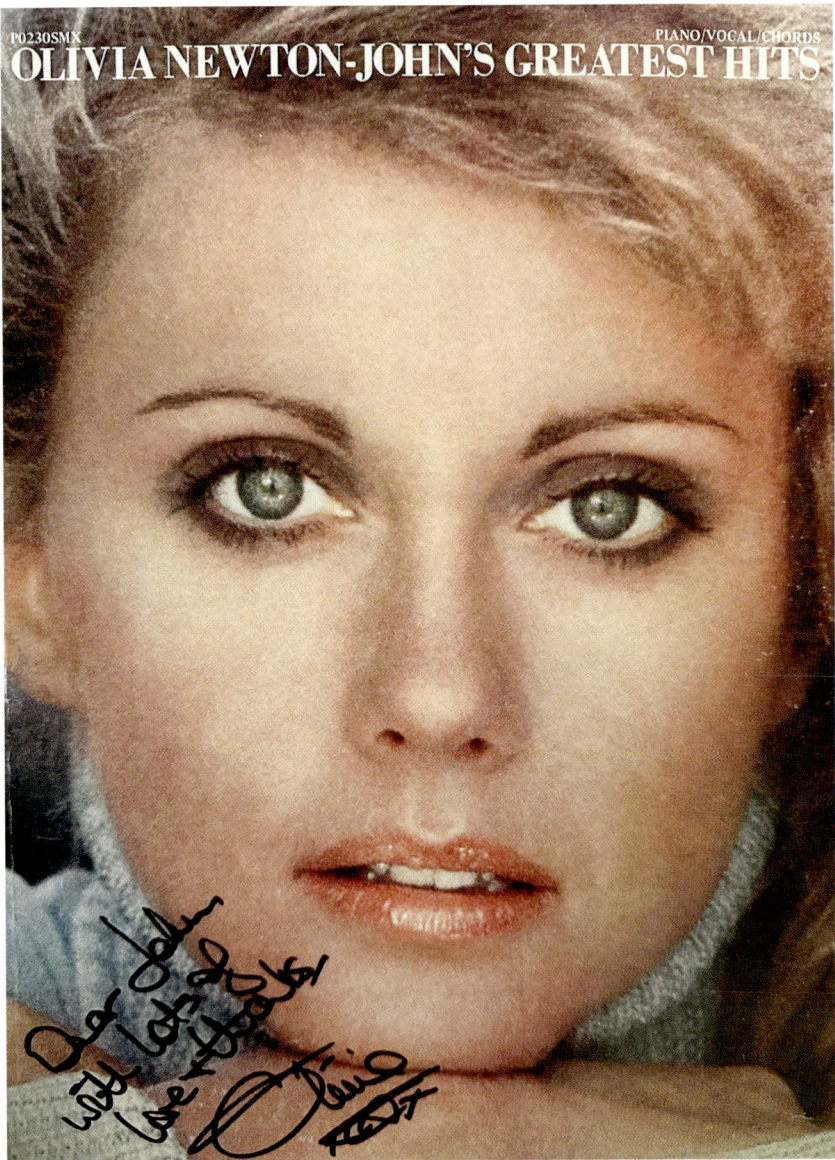

One of my favorite all time photos of Olivia, from way back in 1977.

Olivia Newton-John with her baby, Chloe, then husband Matt Latanzi, and Bianca at our wedding, May 15, 1988.

With Eddie Rabbitt and Tony Scotti.

Primetime television interview with Diane Sawyer for her story on Brian Wilson and psychologist Eugene Landy.

With Jose and Kitty Menendez at our wedding, May 15, 1988.

Brian Wilson with guest at our wedding, May 15, 1988.

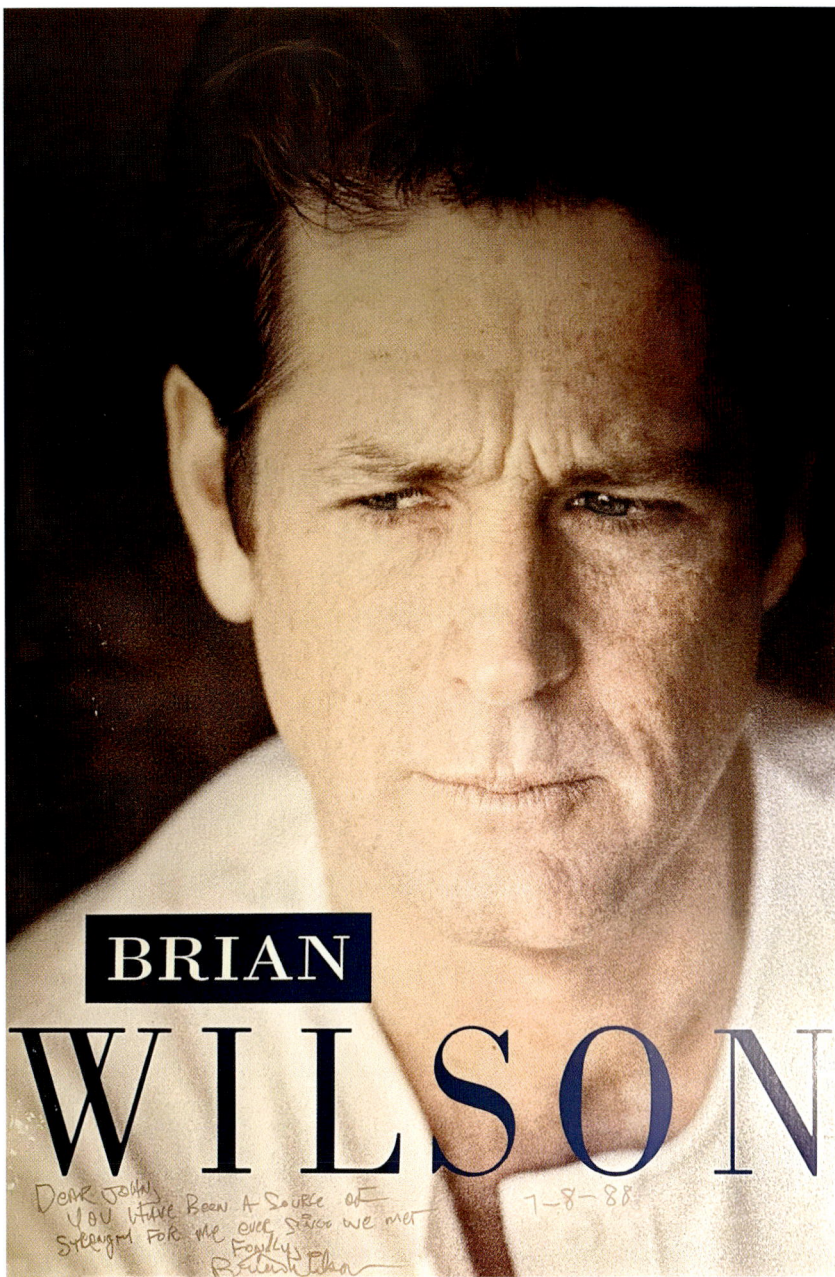

BRIAN
WILSON

"Dear John, You have been a source of strength for me ever since we met.
Fondly, Brian Wilson."

Randy Travis with the Mason family backstage at Harrah's Tahoe. Circa 1995.

Olivia Newton-John with the Mason family backstage at Harrah's Tahoe. Circa 1995.

John and Bianca with Gloria Estefan the night before her Superbowl appearance, Minneapolis, January 25, 1992.

Olivia Newton-John commemorated the 21st anniversary of her amazing turn in *Grease* with a gracious note of thanks. I was on the set the day she and John Travolta shot that iconic scene.

Shakira celebrated her cover profile in Rolling Stone magazine with us in August 2002.

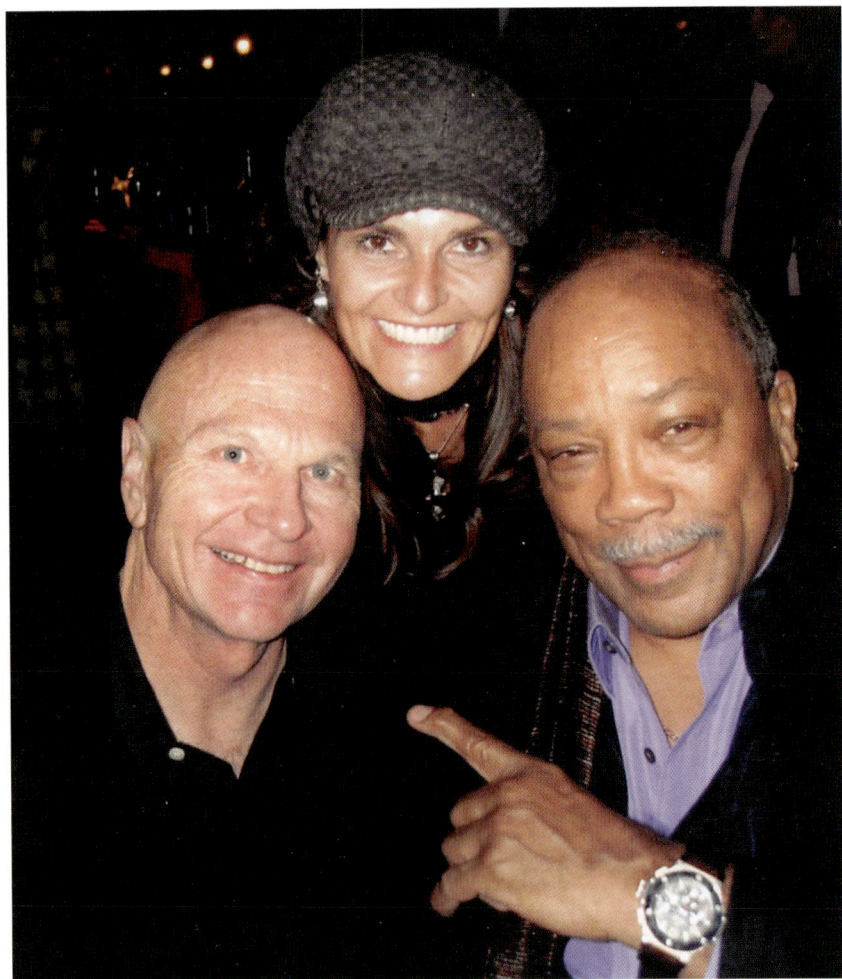

Props from the incomparable "Q". Quincy Jones, circa 1992.

One major thing Kenny had going for him was that even back in the day, he was managed by the amazing Ken Kragen, who would go on to organize the 1985 benefit record "We Are the World" and 1986's Hands Across America. Ken's father, Adrian, was a noted tax expert and my tax professor at UC Berkeley Law. With Kenny's talent and Ken 's flair, they were about to begin one of the most incredibly successful runs in show business history.

✦

Despite having the voice and the drive, Kenny wasn't an overnight success. He started recording in the 1950s with local groups long before becoming a solo artist. Kenny helped form the First Edition in 1967. By 1977, the group had completed their recording obligations at Reprise Records, and the band was having serious disagreements. Kenny moved over to United Artists Records (UA); at the same time, Kragen joined forces with the legendary Jerry Weintraub at Management 3. Weintraub was a force to be reckoned with, but he lacked confidence in Kenny even after Kenny's huge hit at UA, "Lucille."

Finally, out of frustration, Kragen and Weintraub decided to part ways, with Kragen taking Kenny with him. Weintraub basically wanted all the money but not the client, and that's where I came to be Kenny's attorney at the recommendation of Weintraub, who trusted me to be honest and fair.

Kenny had a sophisticated business mind, and he told me he wanted to go with Kragen but didn't want to pay a penny more in commissions than he would have paid if Kragen stayed with Weintraub. Kenny also told me that the real reason he wanted to hire me was because the incoming president of UA, Artie Mogull, told him I would be the "worst choice he could ever make." Kenny laughed when telling me the story and said, "If the president of my label doesn't want me to hire you, I am positive you will be great for me."

Artie was quite a character. He was an old-school record executive who knew great talent and big hits. He would open the UA checkbook and flog the promotion staff to make his choice of records a hit. He did that for "Lucille" and ten more years of hits for Kenny, nearly all of them produced by the legendary Larry Butler.

Funny story, but true: When I became Kenny's lawyer, the president of UA was Mike Stewart, a huge guy weighing more than three hundred pounds. He had to have a special chair and desk made to accommodate his bulk. When Artie came in as president, he took over Mike's desk and chair, but Artie was so tiny, he had to sit in the chair sideways with his legs dangling over the side.

In any event, Artie, Kenny, Ken Kragen, and Larry Butler made hit after hit after hit, which made Kenny one of the biggest stars in the history of the music business. When their formula became a bit stale, Kragen brought in Lionel Richie to write and produce. It worked, and "Lady" topped the pop and country charts in 1980.

Kragen was a hands-on manager and ran the show in every way, but Kenny was a businessman as much as he was an artist. We met every couple of months to "go over everything."

It wasn't long before Kenny was making good money. His team was solid, and he was on tour constantly. Even from day one of knowing him, I could tell that he was one of the great live performers of our time. I've heard he actually performed more than fifteen hundred concerts in his career. I saw at least fifty of them all over the world. Every single show seemed as fresh as the one before, even when they had the same sets and the same bad jokes. Kenny could turn on the showman in him as he walked from backstage to front. Many times, we were actually still talking business as the band started playing. We would pick up right where we left off just after he finished his encore.

The funny thing was his true passion in life wasn't even singing. He loved to buy, renovate, and flip houses. The first one I visited was on Nimes Road in Beverly Hills. The first time I went to Nimes, Kenny introduced me to his beautiful wife, Marianne. He told me how they met on the set of *Hee Haw* and fell in love immediately. Their relationship was magical, and a lot of personal pressure was lifted from Kenny's shoulders when Marianne became involved in the business part of his life as well as becoming the mother of their son, Christopher, in 1981. Every meeting I had with Kenny, at all of his houses, involved Marianne. He usually responded to what I would recommend by looking at Marianne and saying, "Whatever *she* wants."

Kenny and Marianne had a business manager at the time named Mike Gesas, and he dealt with them daily. Artie Mogull and his partner Jerry Rubenstein had purchased UA from Transamerica Insurance and pretty much ran it into a ditch. Artie had a great career as an A&R creative executive, but he wasn't cut out to be CEO or COO of any kind of business.

As the UA contract was coming to an end—and this was after an amazing series of huge hits including "Lady," "Coward of the County," "The Gambler," and "Islands in the Stream"—I told Kragen and Kenny I thought it was time to get off this sinking ship and get on to the biggest record deal ever made. I know that might sound like a major reach, but I really did believe it.

Kenny nodded and said, "Go ahead, but if it isn't the biggest or I don't like the label, it will all be on you."

Kragen told me that Kenny would be going to South Africa to do a huge show at the Sun City Resort. This was during the era of apartheid, but Sun City was technically in a tribal homeland called Bophuthatswana, which enabled all the top entertainers, starting with Frank Sinatra, to perform there frequently. The place had been declared an independent state by South Africa's apartheid government in order to provide gambling and shows banned in other areas of the country. I thought it would be great to have the time with Kenny, Marianne, and even Mike Gesas without all the distractions in Los Angeles, so I went with them.

We were in Kenny's presidential suite at Sun City when I went through every line of the proposal I had put together with Kenny, Marianne, and Mike. Kenny saw stars in those dollar signs. Later, Kenny and I went down to the showroom, where he did another stunning performance. Even his preshow astounded me. Marianne and Mike stayed in the suite playing an intense game of Uno.

Kenny was the ultimate multitasker who could do five things at the same time. He could be talking business, buying or selling a car or some real estate, and then turn around, walk onto the stage, and have the audience on their feet in minutes. When we went back into the suite after the show, Marianne and Mike were still playing Uno, a game they had started about eight hours earlier.

The next day at lunch, Kenny, Marianne, and I started planning our pitch to RCA Records, the label I knew needed a star as big as Kenny, having lost Elvis. Both of them were pros, including in acting, so we thought we could play a Ma and Pa Kettle routine with them on the lawn of their "farm," which was actually a luxury estate called Beaver Dam Farms, a paradise in Colbert, Georgia, complete with a mansion, ponds, trees, ATVs, go-karts, and Kenny's prized pet goat, Smitty. The place was gorgeous and perfect for building relationships.

Kenny wanted a helicopter to take him around on tour, so I put one in the proposal, and we hatched a plan to have all the RCA execs fly in from the Atlanta airport to Kenny's home on a copter we chartered. I put the key RCA exec in the front next to the pilot with the expansive view below him. The other execs I placed in the plush back seats with headsets and more great views. They flew over beautiful Georgia landscapes. As they arrived at Beaver Dam, I had arranged for Kenny and Marianne to be standing on the front lawn waving to them as they landed.

We pulled out *all* the stops.

Staff grabbed the bags and took the execs to various five-star guesthouses, and a fancy lunch was served by the pond. Small pontoon boats were available for the suits to paddle around. Unfortunately, nature didn't always cooperate, and one honcho had a large cottonmouth fall out of a tree into the boat! A few screams later, and this prolific snake was thrown back into the grass, and the exec had a story he would be telling for years. We had a large dinner, and they spent the night. The copter returned the next morning.

After the grand show, I went back to LA to wait, but it wasn't a nail-biter. The record company called me the next day.

"Why don't you come to New York, John?" I was told. "You can get everything you want."

It wasn't long before Kenny signed his new deal, one that was incidentally so big that *The New York Times* wrote about it. Kenny would tell the *Times* reporter he created the whole deal.

It's okay. I'm the back seat guy. I require no credit.

By the way, it was the biggest deal of the day—megabucks back in 1982—plus a helicopter wasn't a drop in the bucket.

✦

From that point on, every record was huge, and Kenny collected his scads of Country Music Association and Grammy Awards while selling out stadiums and arenas on tours that lasted for several years. Network TV specials showcased him, and the fans came out in droves. Hit songs followed hit songs. Kenny even had another number one single with his cover of Bob Seger's "We've Got Tonight," a duet with Sheena Easton. And Kenny wrote a bestselling 2012 biography called *Luck or Something Like It*.

Working with him meant visiting him often at his home in Beverly Hills or Bel Air. There weren't a lot of parking spaces at either house, especially his one house on a hill. I'd try to find a spot and then see Kenny coming home in one of his many cars, including his beautiful black Porsche.

"Kenny, why so many cars?" I asked him once.

"Because I can," he answered.

"If you ever want to sell the Porsche, I would love to buy it," I began.

He ended up selling it to me at wholesale.

That was Kenny, a man among men. He wanted to live forever, and who could blame him? I repped him until '91 as his record career slowed down. We ended around the time Kenny became plastic surgery happy. One night, I saw the "new and improved" Kenny on TV and I almost fell out of my chair. That was a big mistake in my view. You can't really recapture your youth through plastic surgery, although he tried. I do understand getting rid of the wrinkles and the fat, but trying to make yourself look that much younger rarely works.

Kenny's career hit every genre: country, jazz, folk, pop, and even rock. He was one of the most successful crossover artists of all time and bigger than life. I knew him as a big, burly teddy bear of a man. What I remember the most about my friend and client, who passed away in 2020, was this sweet, wonderful guy who was quick with a smile and a warm, throaty laugh and a plan for his next move. There were two Kennys: the superstar and the regular man. I saw both sides, a privilege and honor, plus one hell of a great time.

He knew how to hold 'em. And thrill them.

12
THE MENENDEZ BROTHERS

Just remember what Dad taught us. Master of our emotions. "If I feel fear, I will plunge ahead."
You're a Menendez. You're going to do great things.
—Lyle Menendez

I can't talk anymore. I need to be quiet.
I need to read my Bible.
—Erik Menendez

Even now, twenty-five years since their infamous murder trial, I try not to think too much about the sons of Jose and Mary "Kitty" Menendez. I don't want to get hung up on the story because it breaks my heart. Yet, questions remain: Why did they do it? How could they do it? These are the places I rarely allow my mind to wander. You can get off-kilter if you focus too much on events that really can't be explained unless you probe into dark areas where the real answers lurk.

The Menendez brothers.

Bottom line: They are the only ones who are living who know what really happened. They made up a story of abuse to explain why they fired bullets into the flesh of their unsuspecting parents who gave them everything: life, love, and support, plus the extras, including a posh life in a Beverly Hills mansion, cars, cash, and the best of colleges.

Why murder your parents given all the above? I should have a few clues because I had a unique vantage point as a close friend of the Menendez family. It's why, on those rare occurrences when I do go *there*, I still have to wonder how those two polite boys who sat across from me at countless dinners at the Menendez home grew up to slaughter Kitty and my dear friend Jose. Even the Beverly Hills Police Department didn't think that two entitled kids would do something so destructive.

The cops were wrong.

The police didn't even test Erik's or Lyle's hands for gun residue after the bodies of Kitty and Jose were found blown literally to pieces back in 1996. The brothers weren't suspects, but they were involved in one of the biggest scandals tried weekly in the tabloids.

The nation loves a good whodunit. When you put the city of Beverly Hills into the mix, it becomes irresistible to armchair detectives. The public couldn't get enough of those boys leading the good life and even sympathized with them at the trial . . . until they couldn't anymore. Those two baby-faced brothers who should have been in college were stone-cold killers. They eventually admitted to pulling the triggers but said they had their "reasons." I believe those reasons were fiction and used as excuses or ways to get away with murder, which they did not.

The brothers insisted they committed murder from fear that their father would kill them after they threatened to expose many years of both sexual and emotional abuse. Of course, I wasn't privy to every single moment at the Menendez house, but I spent enough time there with them to call BS on both of those accusations. It took time for the case to unfold, but it wasn't long before I began to see them as two young men who wanted to inherit their father's multimillion-dollar estate. They were impatient. They didn't want to wait for him to die.

The brothers gave him a death sentence.

✦

Jose Enrique Menendez and I bonded quickly and were destined for a long friendship.

He was born in 1944, two years before me, in Havana, Cuba. Jose didn't start out living the good life. As a poor young man, he immigrated to the United States at age sixteen to flee Castro's brutal regime. He got out in the nick of time, along with his parents.

Jose refused to waste his second chance at life. Plus, his parents had a strict work ethic and instilled in him a need to rise to the top. To that end, Jose was not only a successful athlete, but he quickly earned a scholarship to Southern Illinois University. College is where he met a beautiful young woman named Mary Louise, who called herself Kitty, a Miss Illinois beauty pageant winner whose parents did not want their daughter to date "this Cuban immigrant."

Her parents didn't stand a chance against Jose, who was incredibly charming in person. It wasn't long before they were married and on a plane to New York City, where Jose had nabbed a job at a big accounting firm, Coopers & Lybrand. She helped make ends meet working as a teacher while Jose earned an accounting degree from Queens College. Joseph "Lyle" Menendez was born in 1968, which forced Kitty to quit her job. After a move to New Jersey, their second son, Erik, was born in 1970.

One of Jose's big accounts at Coopers & Lybrand was Lion Containers, one of the largest shipping companies in the world. Lion liked him so much that it hired Jose in 1972, and he soon became the president of the company. Hertz hired him next, which is how our futures became linked. At the time, Hertz was owned by RCA, and it wasn't long before hardworking Jose became the CEO of a major record label.

Likely because I had been so active in the television business, I got a call in 1978 from Herb Schlosser, who was president of NBC and, in 1980, would become executive vice president of its parent company, RCA, where he cofounded the TV network A&E, among other projects. He was responsible for the careers of Flip Wilson, Diahann Carroll, Redd Foxx, and others. He also played a key role, in 1975, in the creation of *Saturday Night Live*, a new variety series set to replace weekend reruns of *The Tonight Show Starring Johnny Carson*.

I had just started my own firm, and quickly my practice exploded. I was having a major impact repping artists. Herb thought that Jose should meet some of my influential people on the artistic side.

"I'm moving one of our best executives from Hertz to RCA," he told me. "I'm bringing him out to Los Angeles to meet important people I trust in the music business. I would really appreciate you meeting with him."

I was happy to do it, but I wondered about Jose. How could you move someone from being the CEO of a car company to CEO of a record company? Turns out, you could.

When Jose came to my office, I felt his magnetism, which he exuded with each person in his orbit. He was charming, handsome, intelligent, humble, and funny. He wasn't some slick executive. He told me that he was a Cuban immigrant who was proud of his beautiful wife and sons. I knew he was certain to succeed in building opportunities for them as well as for his employer. There was only one problem. Jose showed up in a suit and tie. I told him neither was allowed in LA, and if he wanted to be accepted and trusted, he had to lose the suit.

This was neither the first nor the last time a corporate owner would put someone with no experience whatsoever in the music business in charge of a record company. The good news was Jose's evident drive. "I'd like to succeed at this job, but I need help. Where can I go for that help?" he asked me.

I said I could help him settle into LA from New York and introduce him to the key people in the artistic community. We attended events together and became friends. When RCA offered Jose a new contract, he asked me to handle the deal. I got him a strong contract, but my advice, as he signed, was to hold on as long as possible, because to this day, every entertainment executive can and *will* be fired at any time. Jose's "boss," Elliot Goldman, was a notorious dictator inside headquarters in New York.

Jose laughed. He did not lack in self-confidence. At the time, losing a job sounded like the worst thing that could ever happen to him.

We had lunch and dinner together often. He always paid, and we always ate at the most expensive showbiz hangouts in LA. He was always extremely generous with gratuities.

With his new contract, Jose was able to move his family to LA and buy a fashionable "mini mansion" in the Flats of Beverly Hills. I remember thinking that they would love being away from those cold winters as they enjoyed the warm California weather. Certainly, his boys would love it—and they did.

They were the all-American family living the California dream.

✦

Shortly after they moved, Jose invited Bianca and me over for dinner to meet Kitty and the boys. Lyle and Erik came into the dining room during the meal to say hello.

Jose was truly proud of the boys and wanted them to have all the advantages and privileges he never had. The brothers were always around when I was over. I loved seeing them, as they were polite, nice kids who had interesting ambitions to make it big, too. In the many times during the day and evening I was at their home, I never heard anyone in this family even raise their voice or say anything inappropriate.

We became family friends who met for dinner once every two to three months. Kitty was lovely, nice, social, and interesting. She enrolled the boys in Beverly Hills High, where Erik's average grades were offset by his remarkable talent as a tennis player, ranking him forty-fourth in the United States for eighteen and under players.

In May 1989, I started planning a surprise birthday party for Bianca's twenty-fifth on June 5. I invited all our close friends, including Jose and Kitty. No one spilled the beans, and when we arrived at a downtown nightclub and walked in, Bianca was in shock. All she could say, even after the "Surprise!" shout, was a happy "What are you doing here?"

Jose decided on the spot to be the champagne sommelier and picked only Cristal, which even in 1989 cost over $100 per bottle. It was generously poured all night, and Jose made sure Bianca's glass was always full, so much so that we had to pull over the limo my friend Carl Parmer had hired. Bianca lost her cookies in a high school parking lot!

Jose paid for the entire night's bubbly. I have no idea how much it was but was relieved not to get the bill! My friend enjoyed his success. I heard from some execs at RCA that he was an aggressive boss, but there was no denying his achievements.

✦

The brothers quickly became accustomed to a privileged life, including the mansion on Elm Drive in Beverly Hills. It was five thousand square feet of opulent decor with a beautiful yard and an expansive swimming pool. Jose rolled around in the latest Mercedes, and the boys had nice new cars as well. Every single time I saw Lyle and Erik, the well-mannered kids said hello. They would sometimes join Jose and me for lunch or even a quick, sweaty tennis game in their yard. The kids didn't work. Their jobs consisted of school and sports. Jose pushed. It was good, but never good *enough*.

"It's motivation. All I can do is try to make sure the kids do the right thing," he told me one day while we relaxed in his yard. R&R wasn't in Jose's blood. He worked constantly and began to amass his fortune.

✦

The buck stops when the company isn't doing well anymore, and the entertainment business is so fickle that you just never know. Even a good year might not be good enough to keep your job, which is why it's musical chairs in those penthouse office suites. As I had predicted the day he signed his contract, Jose was eventually fired by Elliot Goldman when GE took over RCA and pushed the executives to the side. He was actually told that GE would bring in a new president, and Jose didn't want to be subservient, so they fired him.

I set out to help him find a top job in LA entertainment.

At the same time, I knew a lawyer named Peter Hoffman, a brilliant guy who went on to become a producer, through an American independent motion picture company called Carolco Pictures founded by the producers Mario Kassar and Andrew G. Vajna. Carolco would produce three Rambo films, along with hits *Total Recall*, *Terminator 2: Judgment Day*, *Basic Instinct*, *Universal Soldier*, *Cliffhanger*, and *Stargate*. Its downfall was the 1995 film *Cutthroat Island*, which lost $147 million and brought the company to an end.

Jose was there for the solid years of the company as president of its home video division, Live Entertainment. It was Jose who actually turned Carolco into a profitable company within months. I was asked to be on its board while Jose was now chairman of the board. We enjoyed working together and the success after success of the films and video releases.

Jose quickly amassed a wealth that was reported to be around $15 million at the time of his death.

✦

We remained regular dinner guests at the Menendez house. That's how I really got to know the boys. The house was a normal mix of dad always at work and the kids consumed with activities and school. Kitty made sure all of it worked, while also dealing with their social life. Nothing was out of the ordinary except the houses were nicer now, the vacations bigger, and the possibilities were endless.

My possibilities were excellent, too.

In May 1988, Bianca and I got married, and I took the time to reevaluate the rest of my life. The truth was I didn't want to be a big-shot entertainment lawyer anymore, which is why we moved away from LA to Lake Tahoe. The deal was I'd still work by going back and forth to my office in LA when needed and do the rest remotely. It felt good to get away from the hustle of the daily entertainment grind. For the first time since college, I was able to take a deep breath.

Bianca and I would frequently go to LA together. On August 13, 1989, we had dinner with Jose and Kitty at their lovely home, but more about that in a moment.

Seven days later, on August 20, the dream imploded. That evening, Jose and Kitty were relaxing on a couch in the den. Kitty was dozing when Lyle and Erik walked into the room. The only thing out of the ordinary was that they were carrying shotguns. Jose was shot in the back of his head with a Mossberg twelve-gauge shotgun. A groggy Kitty was jolted awake by the shots and stood up from the couch. The boys fired shots in her legs, which caused her to fall backward. That's when they shot her several times in the arm, chest, and face, which left her all but unrecognizable.

The news media reported that it was most certainly a Mafia hit. They stated that Jose probably had Mafia ties. The cops went down the Mafia route because Jose was also shot in the knees, among other places, which said Mafia to them all the way.

Bianca and I heard the news and were devastated. Jose and Kitty were very real and very special to us. I admired my hard-driven Cuban immigrant friend and his beauty queen wife. They had formed a lovely American family. They had it all because they worked for it with determination and dedication. They were at the top of the entertainment industry and enjoyed a gorgeous home in Beverly Hills where they raised their two sons. Their murders in that home were a tragedy beyond anything I had ever experienced in my life.

What about the boys? we wondered.

The two eventually came home that night after going to a local movie theater. They could easily provide their tickets to *Batman* as an alibi, although that wasn't their only stop that night. They had also attended the annual Taste of LA festival at the Santa Monica Civic Auditorium.

It was Lyle who spotted the dead bodies of his parents in the den and called 911.

"Someone has killed my parents!" he shouted into the receiver.

The brothers were not suspects.

A few days later, Erik received some good news that would have made his dad proud. Thanks to my help and for other reasons, UCLA thought he would be a fine addition to its campus and welcomed him into the Bruin family.

The deaths of Jose and Kitty were disgusting and despicable. I jumped right in as a Carolco board member, as we had to immediately deal with the ramifications of our chairman dying, plus complex business issues and the idea of replacing him. I flew to LA and, over the next few days, tried to make things right while also dealing with the pain of knowing that two of my close friends were murdered in their own home.

The theory of a Mob hit was prominent in the news, but it didn't really make sense to me. Why kill Jose? He wasn't involved with organized crime and neither was Kitty. It felt as if the authorities were stretching to tie the case up in a nice bow and not make the murders random. This didn't happen in the tony houses of Beverly Hills. Residents welcomed an answer like the Mob because it meant this couldn't happen to them. The idea that it was a random double murder or perhaps even a robbery had the entire town on edge as security companies were called to double and triple check all doors and windows.

Sitting at Jose and Kitty's funeral felt surreal. Next to me was Jose's sister, Marta, and Kitty's brother, Harold. "We know you were close to Jose and Kitty," Harold whispered to me. "Will you help the boys adjust to life on their own as they heal from this heartbreak?"

"Of course," I promised. "I got their numbers."

By the end of August, the boys were calling me once a week, with Erik more likely to be at the other end of the line. Both wanted moral support and business advice. Lyle had purchased a pizza place after his parents' death. He began to quote me numbers and asked, "Is this a good investment? My dad always trusted you to advise him on all of his deals."

"No, it's not a good idea to own a restaurant," I told him.

Another day, another question.

"Yes, Erik?"

"We bought a condo. Was that a good idea? It's gorgeous," he said.

It didn't seem weird at all. Why live in the house where your parents were murdered? Little did I know that their spending was lavish now. Lyle purchased a Rolex, a Porsche Carrera, and Chuck's Spring Street Café, where he planned to sell Buffalo wings, in Princeton, New Jersey. Erik hired a pricey tennis coach who worked full-time for him and competed in a series of tournaments in Israel. They bought adjoining condos in Marina del

Rey. There were expensive restaurants and a trip to the Caribbean and London.

They did a solid job faking all their emotions about missing their parents. Maybe it was just acting; maybe they did have some remorse. It was enough at this point to outsmart the Beverly Hills police, and I'd always thought of the organization as one of the more sophisticated police forces in the country. In this case, the officers weren't on the right track. Neither was I. As Mob theories persisted, I never dreamed that it could be the boys.

We even talked about them coming to Lake Tahoe to stay at our house.

"I'd do anything for those poor boys," I said to Bianca. (Ironic choice of words because they were definitely not living poor.)

I told Erik, "You'll love it up here. Let's pick a date."

We never did, which you can chalk up to fate or something bigger.

In an odd way, my relationship with the boys felt, for lack of a better word, normal. I knew Jose would have hated the fact that Erik decided not to attend UCLA that September. What I couldn't know then was that Erik would never go to college. He withdrew from the freshman class and began to spend money like crazy.

One day, a few months later, I talked to the detective investigating the case, and we mulled over a few theories including that it was a botched robbery, although none of the valuables in the home were missing.

During this time, Lyle gave a fantastic forty-five-minute interview about his wonderful parents.

He hoped that someday their murderers would be found.

✦

The perfectly mannered boys were arrested on March 8, 1990, a little over six months after their parents were found dead. What did them in was Erik's visits to Jerome Oziel, a local psychiatrist. It turns out that Erik wasn't just there to mull over his grief; he actually confessed to the murders to his psychologist. Legally, the doctor would never be required to discuss what was said due to doctor-patient confidentially laws. Lyle knew this but was still nervous. Just to be sure, he called the doctor and threatened him. The next time Erik visited his shrink, he ran right into the doctor's own plan. Apparently, Oziel had his girlfriend, Judalon Smyth, tape the conversation with Erik, which included another death warning to the psychiatrist. She also told the cops what Erik had confessed to.

People have asked me, "John, how is this admissible?" Answer: Legally, because of the level of threat, Smyth could record the situation. It was as if a third party was overhearing someone's life being threatened. It's not privileged. This third party listening in ultimately resulted in the confession of murder being admitted in court. Judge James Albrecht listened to the tapes between Erik and Oziel and said they were admissible evidence since Lyle had threatened him, which violated doctor-patient privilege.

The police started compiling evidence for the unthinkable, looking at the crazy spending that had occurred since Jose and Kitty died and shifting their focus to the first real suspects they had in the case: the victims' own sons.

The boys were arrested and even admitted that the murders occurred. They said they did it because Jose threatened to kill them for wanting to reveal that they had been sexually abused since they were young children by their father. Kitty just got in the way after they'd shot him, so they claimed there was no choice but to also kill their mother. The brothers insisted that they had no plans to end her life.

Not that it hurt their bank accounts.

There was a will, and they were the sole heirs. With Kitty gone, they boys inherited all of their parents' $14 million, plus a life insurance policy that was worth another $10 million.

✦

Did Jose abuse his sons? I began to push the rewind button. Going back to all those dinners, I remembered him only as a wonderfully charming guy and a great father. Jose was a man's man and a lady's man. He loved his family and their future. There were never any allegations, formal or informal, prior to the arrest of his sons that he abused them or anyone. His and Kitty's deaths were senseless and destroyed everything this family stood for and strived for in life.

I must have been in his presence with his sons more than fifty times and talked to him about his sons hundreds of times. Nothing indicated abuse. Yes, Jose was a hard-driving business-man who pushed strongly to get his way at work and while doing deals. He could be ruthless in business, but he was honest. But at home he was like any other father of teenage sons—a man com-mitted to giving them their best future while keeping them in line and having fun times with them during their teenage years. I never saw him cross any lines. There was nothing hinting at the inappropriate. He was that dad doing everything possible to give his kids the best of the best and providing life's advantages. Sure, he pushed like any other parent. He wanted his boys to excel at school and in sports. He was a Latin dad and knew how hard you had to work to succeed.

The story concocted by Lyle and Erik of sexual and general predatory abuse by their father was and still is absurd to me, compounded by their elimination of the only witness to the slaughter of their father: their own mother. However, it would forever taint the reputations of Jose and Kitty, who was also accused of being an alcoholic. The sons' crime, like many other family murders, will last longer on the public's tongue because patricide and matricide have been considered abominable crimes since the beginning of time. The second tragedy is that while I don't believe the accusations, they are nevertheless there and will remain there forever.

I knew during the court case that I had to keep my focus on my friend, the loving, outgoing executive from Hertz who wanted to make RCA a success again. Jose was put on this earth to make things bigger and better. He didn't just talk the talk but worked the hours and jumped in with an intelligence and business savvy that was formidable.

As the court case dragged on, Kitty's mothering and lifestyle choices were also called into question. I knew her as being a bit more detached than Jose, but by my observations, she was a normal mom in the 90210 zip code who was proud of her sons and happy in her marriage. She was looking forward to the next chapter as the boys launched their own lives and she and Jose became empty nesters.

The lawyers painted a different picture, insisting that Kitty was a detached mother and an alcoholic, although I never saw her drink to excess. It was a glass of wine with dinner, but I never saw her have highballs or martinis.

Erik and Lyle were first tried separately, with a jury assigned to each brother. Then they were tried together with a single jury. I was appalled by the accusations being leveled at Jose by attorney Leslie Abramson, who defended Erik. Jill Lansing was Lyle's lawyer and said in her opening statement, "What we will prove to you is that it was done out of fear."

I flashed back to the first time I met the boys. They were intelligent, athletic young men. Jose would brag that the boys had tremendous potential and how he was prepared to use all his influence and money to help them. To that end, along with Erik's eventual admittance to UCLA, Lyle had been admitted into Princeton. I'm a father of seven. When other people's kids can just talk to me, I know it's a sign of solid parenting.

But something obviously went wrong. Now, the media was talking about if they would get twenty years or life. I felt a chill the day I read a story saying many in Los Angeles and the rest of the country, who treated the story as a soap opera, wanted them to pay the ultimate price. The headline screamed: "Could the Menendez Brothers Be Executed?"

The brothers were found guilty and sentenced to life in prison without the possibility of parole. The California Department of Corrections decided to separate the brothers and send them to different prisons. As maximum-security inmates, their only "perk" was that they were segregated from the other prisoners. In 2018, Lyle was moved into the same prison housing unit as Erik, which marked the first time they saw each other in twenty-two years.

The brothers cried and hugged.

Both were married behind bars. Lyle tied the knot in 1996, marrying Anna Eriksson. She soon found out that Lyle was allegedly cheating on her with another woman. In 2003, Lyle married Rebecca Sneed.

Erik married Tammi Ruth Saccoman at Folsom State Prison in 1999. Their wedding cake was a Twinkie. She told ABC News that her relationship with Erik was "something that I've dreamed about for a long time."

Strange things indeed.

✦

I can't help but think about what happened to my friends. It would come out later in the press that the brothers were fueled by adrenaline. They were upset that night, got their guns, and walked into the room, locked and loaded. They blew their father's head off, and Kitty got in the way. Covered in blood and gore, she ran out of the room and they shot her down.

Years later, Erik would write a short story in jail about a son who comes up with a plan to kill his parents. It was a tale that was on his mind. Some would say that Lyle was actually the one who pushed Erik into murder in real life. It always felt to me as if Lyle was far more aggressive and wanted his dad out of the way. Perhaps they wanted to ditch the stress of being Jose Menendez's son. Perhaps he was more overbearing in private than I ever saw. I'm sure over the last thirty years in prison, the sons of my friend have had enough time to think about what happened on that fateful night.

The shotguns have never been found. If Erik hadn't admitted to the shrink that they'd killed their parents, the court probably wouldn't have been able to convict. The brothers' only link to the murders is a receipt for a shotgun purchased by a friend of Erik's.

There is a story that still goes around that Jose and the boys had a major fight in the days leading up to the murders. The brothers caught wind that their father was going to cut them out of his will and that triggered the tragedy. This, too, seems odd. Why would a dad who adored his sons, who apparently had everything going for them, cut them off? None of it makes sense.

Given the circumstances, we will never know the real truth. It is a $15 million question: Why did they do it? The best I can do is this: I believe they wanted it all . . . now. Jose was clear that he would invest in their education and sports endeavors, but he wouldn't just give them wads of cash, houses, or cars. He would not become a banker to their fancy lifestyle. Instead of buying them a business, he would pay for their degree in business, so they could create a business from the ground up. He would provide opportunities to succeed, but not the spoils of success earned by someone else.

Handing over a lifestyle? That wasn't Jose.

✦

On August 13, 1989, Jose and Kitty hosted a lovely dinner party for Bianca and me at their home at 722 North Elm Drive in Beverly Hills. There were two other couples from the film and music business there. The Menendezes were gracious hosts. The evening started with what else but Cristal champagne and included carefully curated wines with the meal served from their large kitchen next to the dining room. Each of us talked about current and future projects. Around 10:00 p.m., as dessert was being served, Erik and Lyle came in from the garage behind the house through the kitchen to the dining room.

Jose introduced them to the other couples. Everyone smiled and chatted with the brothers. They were nice and polite, as always. Jose asked me to sign a letter endorsing that Erik would be a wonderful addition to the UCLA community and I did. Most of all, Erik wanted to play tennis, and everyone saw real promise for his future as a professional athlete.

It remains unfathomable that we would never see Jose or Kitty again. It remains horrifying to know even now that Lyle and Erik were already planning the murders of their parents and that they would be killed a week later.

It was truly the end . . . of all of them.

13

THE TRUTH ABOUT RANDY TRAVIS
(BE CAREFUL WHAT YOU WISH FOR)

B ack in the spring of 1987, Conway Twitty called, and he was very excited to tell me about this great young country singer who opened for him on the Cruisin' with Conway cruise. He thought I might not have heard of "the Kid"—a.k.a. Randy Travis.

"Conway, this guy has already had three hit singles," I said.

They were "On the Other Hand," "Diggin' Up Bones," and "No Place Like Home."

"Well, he needs a lawyer to renegotiate his deal, and his manager, Lib Hatcher, will be calling you tomorrow."

She did.

I met with Lib and Randy in Nashville the next week, and we got down to business. Back then, Lib wasn't the dominating, intransigent personality she later became in the business or in her personal life, which revolved around one person: Randy.

It was clear to me that Randy was special: shy, introverted, and comfortable with his voice, his record company, and his manager. He was a Southern gentleman in the vein of Elvis, with a quick "Yes, sir" or "Yes, ma'am." It was his standard answer or capper to every question, comment, or compliment. He was deferential to Lib and spoke often, but always softly.

I had no idea back then that there ever was or ever would be a personal or intimate relationship between Randy and Lib. Looking back, there were no overt signs of anything other than this just being business. There was magic in the professional relationship between the young talented country star and the older, more experienced, confident, and hard-charging personal manager.

I bonded with Randy, who loved western art, martial arts, shooting, and riding horses. Me, too! I was also a perfect work match for Lib, with my experience and ability to help her achieve the best for Randy.

He deserved it.

✦

His story could have been a hit country song. He was a string-bean kid who grew up in Marshville, North Carolina, the second of six children of Bobbie Traywick, a textile factory worker, and Harold Traywick, who made his living as a horse breeder, turkey farmer, substitute schoolteacher, and construction business owner.

Book learning wasn't the name of the game here, as young Randy wasn't exactly a fan of school. As a child, he'd skip after the first class. "I didn't like to be told I had to study and had to do homework. There's a fact that you have to want to learn," he said. Later, he would say, "I don't know whether schooling would have helped me get farther along in music at this time. I doubt it would have."

In 1967, at age eight, a guitar-playing Randy took his act pro and played and sang in the Church of Christ choir. A few years later, he joined up with his brother to play local clubs and talent contests as the Traywick Brothers. Randy eventually dropped out of high school, which led to an early life of juvenile delinquency where he was arrested for auto theft, breaking and entering, and burglary.

It was a tough life for Randy, who made some really bad choices early on until music saved his life. A career in petty crime as a teen was put on the back burner after he won a talent contest at a nightclub called Country City USA in Charlotte, North Carolina. That moment would change the trajectory of his entire life, because at Country USA, he met the club's owner, Elizabeth "Lib" Hatcher, who took a deep interest in the young singer and hired him as a cook who would do regular singing gigs at her club. Lib was thirty-seven; Randy was seventeen.

Lib, as she liked to be called, would also end up bailing out Randy after his foolish teenage mind decided to steal a car. The end result was a judge warning him that if he ever showed his face in that specific courtroom again, it would result in a long, long jail sentence.

Then something rather odd happened. Instead of releasing Randy to his already-fed-up parents, the judge decided to put him in the guardianship of Mrs. Lib Hatcher. Yes, she was married, but what's one little marriage when you "adopt" a seventeen-year-old and then decide to become his music manager? You had to give it to Lib, who immediately recognized that Randy was a storyteller and phenomenal talent with unusual and addictive vocal tones. Why not move him into the house with her and her husband?

Meanwhile, Lib kept him busy cooking and singing, so Travis didn't have time to engage in any criminal activities. It wasn't long before Lib left the state of North Carolina. She was looking for a change, so she took her foster child, plus her husband, and moved into a new house in Nashville to start a new life and jump-start Randy's career.

Lib did everything she could to keep Randy working in Nashville clubs. By 1982, the dynamic had shifted dramatically. Lib and her husband divorced, and she could devote more time to Randy, who already had been rejected from every record company in Nashville. My client Eddie Rabbitt was going through the roof, and Travis Tritt was becoming a household name. Kenny Rogers was on fire. Lib kept hearing, "Randy is just 'too country,'" but she refused to give up on him.

Still unable to make any money in the music business, Randy worked as a cook again, and Lib took on the role as a manager of a nightclub called the Nashville Palace. Finally, the fabulous Martha Sharp, who did A&R at Warner Bros. Records, heard him sing live and put a pen in his hand. She had the brilliant idea to hook him up with the producer Kyle Lehning, and the rest became history.

Randy signed with Warner Bros. in 1985 and for a few years still lived hand to mouth. His first single, "On the Other Hand," wasn't the biggest hit, peaking at number sixty-seven on the *Billboard* country charts. Luckily, they put out another one called "Diggin' Up Bones," which was a solid hit, as was "No Place Like Home."

Back in the day, it was thought and drummed into artists that being single and available was important to success. Randy was young, single, and handsome. His recordings were thoughtful, especially for a man. "Diggin' Up Bones" and "On the Other Hand" (both cowritten by my friend Paul Overstreet) had Randy lost and lonely in relationships. Warner Bros. loved and milked that image. By the way, Randy did as well.

Lib? Not so much.

By 1992, his album *Storms of Life* went triple platinum, selling 3 million copies. His second album, *Always & Forever*, came out in 1987 and sold 4 million copies and spawned four hit songs, which all went to number one on the Billboard Hot Country Singles chart.

Thus began years of Randy Travis dominating the country box office. He was the Garth Brooks of the period with hit after hit, a man who would change country music forever while also bringing it back to its roots.

Lib started getting some serious plastic surgery in the hope of looking younger. It worked for her, but it didn't stop rumors that Randy was gay (and he definitely was not) or the crazies who believed they could be "the one." In one case, a woman announced to everyone through letters and media interviews that she was already married to Randy and was coming to Nashville to move in and live with her "husband."

One of the areas of my practice has always been to evaluate all threats and to refer them to the FBI, local police, or private security. This was a constant problem for Olivia Newton-John in her early career and, of course, for Shakira as well. They were hounded by male stalkers. One stalker had Olivia on his personal "kill list."

Randy's alleged wife was the first female stalker I had to deal with, and I was sure she was for real in her intention to come to Nashville and confront Randy. Lib, Warner Bros., and I all contacted the FBI, as she lived in another state and would be crossing state lines. She was caught and sentenced to psychological counseling. Luckily, we never heard from her again.

✦

Lib was a killer businessperson. She learned that I had a really good relationship with Warner Bros. Records president Jim Ed Norman, who had previously been a producer and artist in LA, including working as an arranger for the Eagles, and asked me to renegotiate Randy's recording deal. I was able to get the ball rolling immediately and guaranteed that his profits went through the roof.

Randy sang the hits; Lib ran the show. You could call it an incredible partnership that created a beautiful life for them to share as a couple who lived together. The original husband was out by now.

Lib managed him to perfection, though at one point she hired a business manager named Arlene who was a close friend of hers. Arlene did not know what she was doing, and I had to tell Lib to take her off the team. Lib agreed, and I introduced her to Gary Haber, a trusted business manager. The team was set, and Randy basically signed anything Lib told him to sign.

The bad part about Lib was she offended a lot of people with her strong personality. This included execs from Warner Bros. She kept pushing for extras, like owning the publishing and pushing management commissions up. She wasn't exactly the most popular person in the room.

Based on the crazy stalker incident and the gay rumors, Lib decided they should be married—and they were. Another call on a Saturday night in 1991: "John, it's Lib. Randy's here. We just got married," she said. "We'll announce it to the world next week."

I can't say I saw affection either way, before, during, or after the marriage. They spent all their time together and seemed to get along perfectly well as partners in Randy's career and their many real estate investments. They even bought a few homes in Maui and Hawaii. But the cornerstone and the place Randy loved most was their ranch in Santa Fe, New Mexico. Randy spent his time when he wasn't touring on the ranch, where he liked to shoot guns at his shooting range or bowl in the bowling alley at the house. He would have his fun and then hit the road, where he did mega tours that sold out to the tune of $30 million.

Bianca and I were going to Santa Fe to visit a friend. I mentioned that to Lib, and she said we should come out to the ranch for lunch and a visit. It was stunning, and I thought I saw a relationship, finally. It was close and loving.

Randy ran the tour of the ranch, and it was great to see him enjoy having the things he worked so hard to earn. Awards, outfits, handmade saddles, a gun collection, priceless Native American art, and beautiful, custom-made western furniture were on display. He and I wandered off so he could show me his indoor shooting range and bowling alley. I never saw him happier or more relaxed.

To this day, I have never seen a house this opulent. Yes, wealth and fame can earn those things, but Randy, the juvenile delinquent and dishwasher, the simple guy who liked simple pleasures, would never have asked for this spectacle. It led me to wonder.

"So, unlike Randy to live that way," I told Bianca.

Lib was living out her dream. For Randy, deep down, it may have been a nightmare.

✦

In 1995, I made a deal at DreamWorks Records for Randy to do another album. He had worked with Kyle Lehning on all his hits, but Lib now wanted him to work with someone else. It wasn't the only change in the coming years. We'd later agree he should move back to Warner Bros.

Meanwhile, Lib worried about other women and ultimately had a hidden camera installed in Randy's tour bus to catch him in the act if he was actually cheating. Whatever the falling out was, both of them called to tell me they were getting a divorce. Randy seemed sad; Lib was mad.

Randy told me that Lib would continue as his manager and sort out the financial split. Lib told me the same but added that she wanted a new, long-term contract with a higher commission. I felt the record company, then headed by Jim Ed Norman, should hear from me and not the press that they were divorcing and Lib would continue the management relationship. I told Jim Ed not to worry, that things would remain the same with Lib continuing as manager, me as lawyer, and Gary Haber as business manager. We had been a great team.

Jim Ed said, "We are behind Randy—no matter what."

Lib called me the next day and said, with a venom-tipped tongue, "You had no business telling Jim Ed about the divorce!"

"You and Randy both confirmed the divorce and continuation of management," I said. "I thought it was best to head off rumors and fears of a crisis."

"Well, you're fired," she said. "And since Randy is your client, you should call him to confirm it. Here's his new cell number."

I called Randy, and he was down.

"John, I can't fight Lib," he said. "She told me you could not be my attorney, and I have to do what she says. I could lose everything if I don't."

"Whatever she wants, she can have it," he added. "I just want a divorce."

They ultimately entered into an agreement years later where he gave her everything, and then he challenged the contract. She won in court. The judge held up the agreement.

All that work was truly for nothing, which can leave a man depressed.

As for me, it was the end of my time with Randy. I was out in an instant, but nothing had been resolved. Haber stepped in on the "new" management agreement, even though he still represented Lib and Randy. Lib engineered the divorce and the "settlement agreement." Randy's troubles became public record.

✦

Over time, things got out of control.

In 2012, Randy was found in a parked car in a church parking lot in Sanger, Texas, with an open bottle of wine and smelling like booze. Later that year, state troopers in Grayson County, Texas, got a call that an unclothed man was lying in the middle of the road. It was Randy, who was drunk and had crashed his car into a construction zone. He was arrested after threating the lives of the troopers and was booked for driving while intoxicated and a terroristic threat against a public servant. Cops found that earlier that night, Randy allegedly walked into the Tiger Mart convenience store naked and demanded cigarettes from the cashier, who called the police. He had no money on him and never got the cigarettes.

During all my years working with Randy and being with him hundreds of hours, I never saw him drink alcohol. That had also changed.

But that wasn't the worst of it. In July 2013, Randy found himself in a Dallas hospital, where he was diagnosed with viral cardiomyopathy, an upper respiratory infection. He was in critical condition and then suffered a massive stroke

Paul Overstreet, who wrote so many hit songs for Randy, and I visited him at Vanderbilt University Medical Center in Nashville. Everyone, including his doctors, thought he wouldn't make it. This strong, handsome, and amazing man was comatose and unresponsive at one point. He weighed maybe one hundred pounds.

Surgery to relieve pressure on his brain helped, but for a long time, he couldn't walk or talk. Despite physical therapy, he would need to use a cane for over a year. He even had to relearn the guitar with the help of his fiancée, Mary Davis, who would become his next wife. Mary was with him through the entire ordeal. She still is.

Randy remembers a lot. Maybe everything. He just can't (or won't) talk about it. I talk to him occasionally and still see everything in him that his fans and I love.

Same guy, start to finish, except for the years in between.

✦

A decade after the divorce, I was subpoenaed to testify in a case where Randy was the plaintiff and Lib the defendant. I had not seen either of them for years. Randy came in early, and I was delighted to see him, even though he was still seriously physically and vocally challenged by the stroke.

It was extremely difficult for him to speak, but he was fully mentally capable. I asked, "Randy, why are we here?"

"Lib got everything and I got nothing," he said.

I certainly don't know if that was true, and I never heard what happened with the case. I also spoke with Lib that day. She was gracious and friendly. Not much had changed. At the same time, everything had changed. The magic was gone.

The fight was over what was left.

✦

At the Country Music Hall of Fame in October 2016, Randy Travis sang "Amazing Grace," and there wasn't a dry eye in the house. But a comeback was not in his future. His right hand didn't work and his speech was limited. The stroke impaired his ability to sing. He could make public appearances, but the show was truly over despite an announced twelve-city tour, which ended after three cities.

His last song was "Fool's Love Affair," released in 2020. It sounded like the old Randy and it was. He admitted it was recorded in the beginning of his amazing career.

Lib enjoys some of the royalties.

My friendship, as it should, continues with both.

14

EDDIE RABBITT MAKES IT RAIN

Once in a blue moon, everything will be right with the man in the sky, and when I start singing "I Love a Rainy Night," from out of nowhere, there will be lightning and thunder. I just say, "Folks, we've got the best special effects guy in the world, so let's get wet together."
—Eddie Rabbitt

I wrote earlier in this book about how hard it was to get that first job in entertainment law. About nine months before the call from the Kaplan firm, I got an offer (which I accepted) from a tax and estate planning firm in Beverly Hills with, at least, some clients in the entertainment business. Bob Crane, star of the hit TV series *Hogan's Heroes*, comes to mind. I never got to work on his account, but the firm represented some great financial investors in Bakersfield, California. Their principal investment? Cows!

One of these Bakersfield guys had a friend, Dave Bell, who had been a Bakersfield cop but had big dreams. Bell came into the office to meet me (and I was still only a first-year lawyer with no real training or skills).

"I want to get into the record business," he said, "and I know just how to do it."

Bakersfield in those days rivaled Nashville as the "home of country music," with Buck Owens, Merle Haggard, Fuzzy Owen, Ferlin Husky, and Barbara Mandrell, among many others, contributing to the "Bakersfield sound." Bell told me there was a record company based in Nashville named Mega Records, owned by an insurance company that wanted out of showbiz. (How? It probably involved a misguided tax plan.) Mega had one huge hit, "Help Me Make It Through the Night," by Sammi Smith, but was losing money hand over fist.

"Let's get to Nashville and see if we can buy it," Bell said.

I jumped at the chance to go to Nashville for the first time to get some experience and to maybe have my first real client. One question remained: Why would a retired Bakersfield cop with no money think he could buy a record company in Nashville? Three keys: Dream big. Believe in yourself. Be a great bullshitter.

Our first day in Nashville, we went over to Mega and met both of its two employees: Brad McCuen, who served as president, and Jim Malloy, the vice president of A&R, who had produced and won a Grammy for the Sammi Smith hit. Bell and I were successful in his acquisition of Mega, but there was no money for staff, so McCuen and Malloy had to leave. Fortunately for me, Malloy became a close friend and my second client. He had never been paid a royalty, but he was incredibly talented and a great scout of music and artists. I helped him start a publishing company, and his first two songwriters were Even Stevens and his son, David Malloy. They were working with another Nashville writer and would-be recording artist, a guy named Eddie Rabbitt. His career, up to this point, had been more downs than ups.

The trio of Even, David, and Eddie, now all in the Country Music Hall of Fame, had no doubt of their talent and surely had no lack of enthusiasm. We all met up to get the ball rolling at Eddie's little rented house on a Saturday back in 1974. I know it was a Saturday, because Eddie had a small monkey, which appeared to have ADHD. It lived in a very large cage in Eddie's dining room where normally there would be a table for eating (he didn't have one, or any other furniture to speak of, either). It turns out the monkey, JoJo, was a big fan of *Hee Haw*, which came on in Nashville at 5:30 p.m on Saturday.

We had started talking about songs and opportunities at about 4:00 p.m. Around five o'clock, JoJo started going crazy, jumping all over the top and bottom of the cage. We asked Eddie if JoJo was okay. "Yeah, he gets really excited when *Hee Haw* is coming on," he said. Apparently, the monkey loved the blond girl in the opening sequence, because when she came on he just "got romantic." Clearly, Eddie's future wife, Janine, didn't like JoJo or his affinity for *Hee Haw*, and the monkey disappeared as soon as they were formally engaged.

✦

When we first started working together, Eddie was frustrated that he'd had to give up a potential record deal because of his song "Kentucky Rain." His prospective record company said, "You record that song or you're out."

"Listen, son, Elvis will record that song," Colonel Tom Parker said. "But you have to give up the publishing."

When you're struggling to pay the rent and feed your monkey, the choice becomes urgent. Whether "Kentucky Rain" would have been a hit by Eddie, we will never know, because he chose Elvis over Eddie. In hindsight, it was a great choice, because the Elvis cut is a classic, and Eddie had many bigger hits over the next twenty years. His later recording of "Kentucky Rain," in my opinion, is far better than the one by Elvis, but remember Elvis cut everything on short notice. Eddie had decades.

So, Elvis took "Kentucky Rain," and Eddie worked in a pizza joint in Tullahoma, Tennessee. He was so frustrated with his "non-career" that he signed an exclusive, long-term management agreement with the owner of the pizza place. He also signed an exclusive record contract with Grand Productions, the little, not-so-grand company formed and funded by Jim and David Malloy so they could spend their own money and develop talent. Incredibly, Jim and David never pushed Eddie to sign with them as a songwriter, so his own Briarpatch Music owned all his shares of his songs until he sold it in 1986 to MTM Records, cofounded by the amazing Mary Tyler Moore and her then husband, Grant Tinker. That deal made Eddie rich, but it didn't change his lifestyle.

So, there was a puzzle to be solved: an iron-fisted manager with no experience or contacts in music and a record contract with no distributor. What did Eddie do? He wrote "Pure Love" for Ronnie Milsap and "Tullahoma Dancing Pizza Man" for the manager, who was so flattered I was able to get him to release Eddie for $10,000. The next step was to get him a record deal with my friend Steve Wax at Elektra/Asylum Records in LA. Steve, one of the greatest promo radio guys of all time, truly believed in the potential of "country crossover."

Eddie defined it. The Rabbitt, Malloy, and Steven team would go on to have country hits and Top 40 crossovers such as "I Love a Rainy Night," "Drivin' My Life Away," and "Suspicious." Sounds easy? It wasn't. This was long before Taylor Swift.

The direct deal I made for Eddie with Steve gave Eddie an amazing royalty, a great recording budget, as well as the chance to be on the radio immediately. However, his first singles weren't hits. Steve didn't give up, and in 1976, "Drinkin' My Baby (Off My Mind)" hit number one on the country charts. Several more country hits followed, and by 1980, the singles "Drivin' My Life Away" and "I Love a Rainy Night" were giant pop hits as well.

I saw in Eddie a special artist, a great songwriter, and an amazing performer. Even though he was in Nashville with Tennessee-based cowriters and producers, his music came from New Jersey bars. I believed early on that he could have pop hits as well as country ones like "Two Dollars in the Jukebox" and "Drinkin' My Baby (Off My Mind)."

Back when I asked Mike Curb about a job at MGM and found out that he was already gone, he suggested I meet his brother-in-law Tony Scotti, who had been an A&R executive and actor. Tony's brother, Ben, was considered the best promo exec in the business. When they left MGM, they started Ben Scotti Promotion. They were Italian, and a rumor started that they were in the Mob. They weren't. They were the real deal and promoted artists on every label and any genre to the tune of hit records. Clients ranged from Abba to Barbra Streisand.

Shortly after leaving MGM, they decided to also start a management company and brought in MGM's head of A&R, Stan Moress, to run it. Since Curb had introduced us, I went to their office on Sunset Boulevard to try to get them to hire me as their attorney. I ended up walking out believing Stan, Tony, and Ben could be the keys to breaking Eddie. How right I was!

The Scottis knew Steve Wax (another New Jersey guy), who had been hired by the former president of Warner Bros. Records Joe Smith to be president of Elektra/Asylum Records (founded by Bob Krasnow and David Geffen, respectively) when the two labels merged. Joe in his infinite wisdom asked Steve to create a country record division from Los Angeles. So, the Scottis sent me to Steve. He got it with Eddie and started the hit machine that brought us "Drivin' My Life Away," "I Love a Rainy Night," and "Suspicious."

Steve was a "wild and crazy guy" who died far too young. Frankly, to me, working in music in LA in the '70s and '80s, cocaine was enemy number one. Steve, Eddie Rabbitt, Neil Bogart, and countless other artists, writers, and executives are not with us today who should be.

✦

When I wrote earlier that money didn't change Eddie Rabbitt, I failed to mention that success and stardom did.

Stan Moress was the perfect manager for Eddie (and also had succumbed to some white powders on occasion). With Ben Scotti and Steve Wax on the team during promotions, Eddie exploded. In my experience with him, Eddie never changed. He was super kind and super funny. He was the guy with the monkey and the girls, until he met and married Janine Girardi in 1976. She was the one he called "a little thing about five feet tall, with long, black beautiful hair, and a real pretty face." He wrote "Sweet Janine" for her. They would have three children: Demelza, Tommy, and Timmy, who tragically passed away at twenty-three months due to complications after a liver transplant surgery.

Janine was a great influence on Eddie and brought him back to earth from his escapades and solitary life. The Rabbitts purchased a farm outside Nashville, which was Eddie and his wife's pride and joy.

At the same time, Eddie became paranoid about his fame and started wearing disguises, even in Nashville. I will never forget his call to ask, "John, you're from LA. Where can I get costumes and makeup so no one will recognize me?'"

"Eddie, nobody in LA wears costumes and makeup," I said.

So, he found someone in Nashville and went everywhere with a fake beard, even though he had a real one, plus he wore a wig. He had dress-down clothes no entertainer would ever wear in public. I didn't think it was anything other than eccentricity until we met after the Houston Livestock Show and Rodeo in 1984 for our annual "State of the Rabbitt" meeting, a planning and review session. I do these to this day with clients.

It was a huge show in the Houston Astrodome in front of sixty-eight thousand people. Eddie had the presidential suite in an adjacent hotel, and his manager, business manager, agent, and I went up to get set for a midnight meeting. Eddie came up an hour or so later, took a shower, and changed. When he came out and joined us, he was in great spirits.

"Hey, guys," he said. "Where's the cocaine?"

I was in shock. An envelope came out filled with white powder, which was poured onto the table.

"Hold on, guys," I said. "This is illegal, and I am a lawyer. I can lose my license if anyone, including room service, walks in."

I got some strange looks.

"Okay, you can either join us," Eddie said, "or leave."

I left.

Eddie and I did not speak to each other for a year. I didn't quit and wasn't fired. For that year, I spoke with his manager, agent, and business manager as if nothing ever happened. When Eddie and I reconciled a year later, that incident was not discussed or ever mentioned again. It was just a sign of the times, or for me, a cautionary tale. Only one other person in the room that night is still alive. Steve Wax has been gone for decades.

✦

One day in 1981, Jim Malloy called me to say he had found "one of the great ones" in a song called "You and I." Jim said it was one of the best he'd ever heard. It was written by a new, young songwriter named Frank Myers. Frank needed money, but Jim didn't want to sign him to a long-term contract. So, he bought the song for $100, plus a decent royalty, and asked Eddie to record it. Eddie loved it and saw the potential for another huge crossover hit. He called me and said, "John, I know this can be a big hit, but I need to record it with Barbra Streisand. Do you know her?"

I didn't, but I did know her manager, Marty Erlichman. I called him. He passed. I called Eddie to let him know and then offered to ask my client Crystal Gayle to record it. Eddie met her in a studio and the rest is history. It became the number one wedding song of all time.

Funny thing, in every show Eddie ever did after 1981, he told the story of how he thought of Crystal the moment he heard the song.

✦

It's strange how things change over time. In 1986, though we hadn't spoken for a year, I knew I could make a new deal for Eddie where he could own his masters and get a boatload of money. RCA (where I had also moved Kenny Rogers) was willing to make the leap of faith. Two albums later, the label wanted out. New management always does that. They fire staff, cut artists, and move on, blaming the last administration while cutting costs.

Eddie was still a star, but his records had lost their fire. In reality, the era of the country crossover was over. Eddie handled it well. He loved his family and his life. He still had huge shows and enough money and income to support his lifestyle.

In 1997, he was diagnosed with lung cancer. He had been a heavy lifelong smoker. Janine did her best to get him to stop, but he didn't. Eddie went to the hospital for treatment and never got out. I will never forget my last conversation with him. He called me on my mobile phone and sounded so weak I could barely understand him.

"John, I am going to die. Very soon," he almost whispered. "I don't mind not being here anymore, but I am devastated that my kids will lose their dad."

Eddie died on May 7, 1998, of lung cancer. He was fifty-six.

15

OUT OF THE DARKNESS AND INTO THE LIGHT (GLORIA ESTEFAN)

All of your dreams can come true,
if you have the courage to pursue them.
—Walt Disney

will never forget the first time I met Gloria and Emilio Estefan. I was introduced to them by phone in 1985 by my friend Stan Moress. He also repped Eddie Rabbitt, Clint Black, Tammy Wynette, Donna Summer, and others, including the Miami Sound Machine, whose album *Eyes of Innocence* produced their first hit, "Dr. Beat."

Emilio had big dreams and Gloria had big talent. A win-win.

In August, they asked me to come down to their Miami office, and frankly, I had never been to Miami nor had I represented any Latin talent. Emilio gave me the address, and when I got there, to my surprise, it was a little house on a small lot. The garage door was open. Inside the garage was the "office" of the Miami Sound Machine, and I spotted Emilio in there along with Gloria's sister, Becky, and Emilio's older brother, Jose. Inside the house were Gloria and her mother, Big Gloria, who watched over everyone and offered copious rounds of strong Cuban coffee. It was delicious.

Back in the garage, there was fan mail and boxes everywhere. I found out that Becky was Gloria's assistant, while Jose and his wife, Patti Estefan, were the business managers. Emilio was the ringmaster, and Gloria was the star. I knew how determined they were to make it big. No one spends long days and nights in a hot Miami garage toiling away if they aren't serious. What struck me the most was that they were an amazing immigrant family with a positive outlook despite hardships in life. There was a collective spirit and can-do mentality that told me that nothing would get in their way. Talk about a family business!

By the time I visited the Estefans' "office," Miami Sound Machine's ninth studio album and second English-language record had come out with the single "Conga." Gloria's vocals and the distinctive sound of the group pushed the single to the top of the charts, along with the ballad "Words Get in the Way." Yet, it was "Conga" that launched a revolution and changed the lives of the entire family and the future of Latin music.

Gloria became a superstar, but she has not changed to this day. A hardworking mom then and now, she was writing and recording incredible songs while also washing clothes and dishes.

I was hired on by Emilio as their attorney, I heard "Conga" so many times at so many great shows that I would sing it in my sleep. (Even now, just thinking about that tune makes most people want to get out of their seats and dance.) The cut was huge, and it was a showstopper at their live shows, which through word of mouth were becoming must-see events.

Everything exploded at that point, and they moved out of the garage. Emilio, ever the businessman, as well as producer and manager, found a small building in Miami Beach and turned it into a hit-making factory with a kick-ass recording studio and a top floor full of offices. Crescent Moon Studios was born. Emilio stocked the place with a dozen talented, full-time employees, as well as songwriters, artists, and producers. These artists ranged from Jon Secada to Shakira.

Nearby, they bought a lot on Star Island and built a beautiful home on the water with a dock and a boat the likes of which I had never seen, but more on that later.

Back in those days, Stan Moress had been Gloria's manager for several years, but I don't remember ever seeing him at the garage or in the Crescent Moon offices. Because Emilio was brilliant and driven, it seemed inevitable that Emilio would take over and Stan would be phased out, which is exactly what happened. The issue was Stan didn't want to go. He sued Gloria and Emilio, and a war began. It didn't affect Gloria's career at all. She flourished, but the litigation, which I didn't participate in, cost both sides a boatload of legal fees. Sadly, it got really personal with Stan, who claimed he was the mastermind. Emilio stated in a public deposition that the only positive thing he could say about Stan was that "he wore great socks."

The case settled as Gloria's and Emilio's careers exploded.

Emilio discovered and signed some truly great writers to his company Foreign Imported Productions and Publishing. This was a phenomenally successful business plan, with the songs 100 percent owned by the Estefans.

I didn't see Gloria often at the office, but each time I went to Miami, she and Emilio invited me out to dinner or over to their house. Originally, their lot on Star Island didn't look that big to me, but the house they built there was large and stunning. It was also a comfortable home for their son, Nayib, to live in with his famous parents and Big Gloria. Their neighbors would someday include Jennifer Lopez, Sean "Diddy" Combs, athletes, and various business executives.

My meetings with Gloria were conducted in the house because she was, above all, a mother first. She was still able to write incredible songs and record them during the evenings while her son was in bed and being watched over by Big Gloria. When daughter Emily came along, Gloria was ecstatic to have a little girl.

There was plenty of time to enjoy their new life.

I was outside their house on Star Island when I spotted Emilio's newest toy, a cigarette boat, which was parked at his private dock. He suggested that Bianca and I should go for a ride the next time we were in town, and so we did. Once in open water, we were soon skating across the surface at seventy miles an hour. As the mist of Biscayne Bay flew in my face, my contact lenses stuck to my terrified eyes. I couldn't blink or see anything the entire ride. Clearly Gloria and Emilio loved it. I, on the other hand, had never been on such boat and vowed never to do so again.

Gloria and Emilio continued to create hit after hit with lyrics that were somehow more and more inspired. Emilio always invited me to the studio if they were recording. I was there when they recorded "Anything for You" and "Rhythm Is Gonna Get You" for the album *Let It Loose*. By 1989, Emilio made an executive decision and dropped "and Miami Sound Machine" from the group's name. It was just Gloria Estefan now.

Gloria has a stunning voice. Her amazing words and vocals on "Cuts Both Ways" knocked me out when Emilio first played it for me. It would stand the test of time and remains a classic to this day. Another plus for Gloria is that she has one of those voices where you know it when you hear it—and that's what *it* is. That's what it takes to be different, to be better than the other talented singers with hits but not careers.

Speaking of voices, Emilio's is unique as well. With his strong Cuban accent and effervescent enthusiasm, he wins over the skeptics. He surely won over Tommy Mottola at CBS Records (now Sony), who believed 100 percent in Gloria and later Shakira and brought the money and power to back and break their careers.

Gloria has evolved as a writer and a person. She is no longer the shy girl I met all those years ago but an accomplished singer-songwriter who is part of this amazingly creative partnership with her husband. She has also graduated to superstar level, yet during my time with her, I saw that being a mother to her kids was the biggest priority. How is it possible that she hasn't changed? She is the same person I met in that garage despite money, power, and the ability to sell out arenas. There's no ego, no demands, no drama.

I was determined, while writing this book, to provide an unvarnished look at my clients' lives and careers. As I thought about Gloria and Emilio, I had to conclude they are and always have been the same family and friends I met in the garage decades ago, despite the success and relentless touring schedules.

As for the shows, Emilio and Gloria thought *big*. The sets for the tours cost millions. There were no Live Nation or AEG deals back then. They bet on themselves and won.

The tours were lengthy and wonderful, but so were nights at home just watching movies with the family. Gloria was bubbly and fun—a role model and a confidante, an amazing talent and a down-to-earth, grateful person who didn't take any of it for granted.

Her positivity would help her survive one of the worst moments of her life.

✦

On March 20, 1990, the Estefans were on their tour bus going from Pennsylvania to New York. They had one of those tricked-out Prevosts, a luxury custom motorhome with a large, private bedroom as well as a bunk for their ten-year-old son, Nayib (Emily had not yet been born). It started to snow. The storm was so severe that after an hour or so, the driver had to pull over on the side of the road. An eighteen-wheeler suddenly bashed into the bus while Gloria was in the back napping. Later, she would recall that it "felt like an explosion. It was huge." The impact threw Gloria from her bed to the floor.

Emilio was also on the bus, along with Nayib. Covered in his own blood, Emilio found the strength to run to Gloria, hover over her, and scream, "Are you okay?"

Somehow, Gloria knew that she had broken her back. She even tried to stand, but later reported, "I had the taste of electricity in my mouth. That's the only way I can describe it. The pain was excruciating." Meanwhile, Emilio was screaming out for their son, but there was no answer. Gloria recalled, "I kept praying to God. 'Please, Lord, let him be OK. I don't care if I'm paralyzed. I don't care what happens to me. Please let him be OK.'"

In that mayhem, Nayib was found with a broken clavicle, and he was taken to his mother. He begged her to stand. All Gloria could do was tell her boy that it was going to be fine.

The diagnosis was that Gloria's spine was broken. Her situation was so bad that she could barely breathe. Doctors told her that she might not regain the use of her legs and that she would no longer be able to have children.

It was ski season in Lake Tahoe, where I was living at the time with my family, when I saw the accident flash across the news. It was close to midnight on the East Coast, nine or ten in Tahoe, and I called Emilio on his cell. He answered right away. He really couldn't say more than one sentence: "John, I'm praying for her."

"I'll pray for her, too," I told him.

What the public didn't know was that three weeks later, it was still touch and go. Bianca and I went to visit Gloria in the hospital, where she was gutting it out but grateful to be alive. I had never seen her in distress, and now here she was, drained of all her energy and in excruciating pain. However, as always, her attitude was positive. "I can't wait to get out of here and back to my family." She even joked around and told us, "At least I have time to write some new songs."

Over the next months, she got better and better. The pivotal day was when she started walking again thanks to the two titanium rods that were implanted to stabilize her spine. After the operation, she found the inner strength to do a year of serious rehab work in and out of the hospital until she was not only able to walk freely but was given a green light to tour again.

I've witnessed several miracles in this life, and this was definitely one of them.

How she recovered could only be called God's grace. God's blessing. Emilio was hurt, but not like her. Later, we would joke that they were truly the couple who did *everything* together.

By 1991, she was fully back at work and wrote the gorgeous inspirational ballad "Coming Out of the Dark" about her near-death experience. In 1992, she defied all the odds and was the halftime entertainment at the Super Bowl in Minneapolis. For obvious reasons, I had never been to Minnesota in the winter, but Gloria and Emilio invited us. Let me just say that there were ice sculptures there that never melted . . . not even one drop.

I was on the sidelines and in the dressing room while she prepped for her Super Bowl performance. And then I was on the field at sound check. I was still standing on the field when the teams came running out to warm up. I never knew how big those guys were until they were right there in my face. They began to run out onto the field and we had to get the hell out of there. It was a great experience and a big show. That night, Emilio and Gloria hosted a huge party in their hotel suite to celebrate. It was just wonderful.

The other happy news was that I was able to renegotiate Gloria's contracts until they were works of art. Gloria and Emilio own all their songs.

By 1993, Gloria wanted to get back to her Hispanic roots and did her first Spanish-language album, *Mi Tierra*, and then a beautiful holiday album called *Christmas Through Your Eyes*. Bianca and I spent Christmas with them before their daughter, Emily, was born in 1994. Yes, she was able to have another child, which was another miracle. It was a wonderful experience being a part of their family for the holidays.

Emilio was also producing many other artists by then, including Shakira, who would also become my client. Emilio had his own in-house everything. From his first job selling rum for Bacardi to running a virtual empire, Emilio kept learning and succeeding. Hotels, restaurants, commercial real estate, music, theater, and movies seemed to come naturally. Throughout our time together, I found Emilio to be a really funny, really smart man who was accessible to everyone—as is Gloria, a woman with three Grammys and fifteen Billboard Latin Music Awards.

They're just real people . . . if everyone had a spectacular career, plus a restaurant called Estefan Kitchen in Orlando and two hotels. It's a giant success story built by people with integrity who know how to get things done. She's a brilliant musician; he is a driving force. Most of all, they're just beautiful people.

I haven't seen a change in Gloria or Emilio, who both still have the same cell phone numbers and answer their phones themselves to this day. I remember them introducing me to Joe's Stone Crab, a restaurant in Miami with locations in other cities. It's the kind of place with a long wait for a table, maybe three hours during peak times, which is exactly when we went there. I learned that when you're with Gloria and Emilio, there is no wait and you get the best table.

The stone crabs are pretty good, too.

16

BARRY MANILOWS AND HIGHS

No one person or material thing could ever come close to the feeling I get when the music is right.
—Barry Manilow

What do Janis Joplin and Barry Manilow have in common? The answer is Clive Davis. The legendary head of Columbia, CBS, Bell, Arista, and RCA Records called me in 1973 to invite me to a showcase at the Troubadour on Santa Monica Boulevard in Los Angeles to see and hear the incredible first artist he intended to break wide open at Bell, after being unceremoniously fired in the middle of a brilliant career at CBS Records.

His name was Barry Manilow.

I will never forget Barry's stellar performance that night on the tiny ten-by-twelve Troubadour stage. It was standing room only because there were no seats on the floor of the place. Of course, that makes it easy to get a standing ovation! Barry knocked out everyone with a show that was electric. He killed with those smooth vocals and lyrics that tugged at your heart and stirred your soul. It was actually the perfect place for a guy with a piano. Of course, Clive knew that.

Back when Clive introduced us, Barry had terminated his relationship with his original manager and was transitioning to the incredibly talented Garry Kief, who was introduced to me by my friend Barry Krost, manager of Cat Stevens. I remember meeting Garry backstage and thinking how incredibly handsome he was and how his blue eyes and black hair created the look of a movie star. However, behind the vision was a visionary. Somehow, Garry saw, predicted, and conquered image building.

Garry and I hit it off. He said if Barry approved, he would like to bring me in as Barry's lawyer. He set up the meeting in my office in Beverly Hills, and this started a decades-long friendship and legal partnership.

✦

First, a little background. Barry grew up in Brooklyn, a kid who liked to sing and write songs. He began his career when the CBS director Bro Herrod asked him to arrange some songs for the musical adaptation of the play *The Drunkard*. Barry didn't just write a song or two. He wrote the entire score.

Barry was actually "discovered" first by my friend and client Tony Orlando, then a songwriter, artist, and producer who also served in A&R at Columbia Records. In fact, Barry and Tony started a studio group called Featherbed. Never heard of it? Neither did I nor anyone else. They weren't "good enough" for Columbia, so Tony signed Barry to the Columbia Pictures–owned label Bell Records.

Shortly after forming Featherbed, Barry was again "discovered," in 1971, by the Divine Miss M, Bette Midler. They had a great run at the Continental Baths in New York City, while Barry simultaneously became the king of jingle writers, producing songs for companies including Pepsi-Cola, State Farm Insurance, and McDonald's ("you deserve a break today"). Who knew?

Still, it came as a big surprise to me, back in 1973, when Clive decided to bet the farm and his career on this talented, but unknown, pop and commercial artist who had never written or recorded a hit single. Then along came "Mandy," which launched Barry's career. Barry didn't write it and, famously, did not want to record it. However, as the saying goes: What Clive wants, Clive gets. Same for "I Write the Songs." Barry didn't write it but made it sing! Both were huge hits.

✦

Garry was the perfect manager and life partner for Barry. He understood Barry and his music. While I saw Barry often at Garry's Stiletto Entertainment office on Sunset Boulevard, he never actually participated in a business meeting. Barry always dressed impeccably and listened in as Garry and I negotiated incredible deals for Barry with Clive, who continued to push Barry to hit after hit. This included discovering Bruce Johnston's amazing "I Write the Songs."

When Clive folded Bell into his new label, Arista, we did Barry's Arista deal, which was great for Barry. There was no reason for him to ever leave. Funny thing: Maybe Clive was as mesmerized by Garry as me. Wow, when you can focus and still drill down, it's remarkable how much can be achieved. Garry and I planned carefully, and Clive made the deal.

Meanwhile, the tours never seemed to stop and the songs kept racing up the charts as Barry's fan base exploded. He and Garry created a success machine. Barry was a born showman, in addition to being a great songwriter, musician, arranger, producer, and singer. He tore it up at every single show.

I have had a direct personal relationship, effectively daily, with all my clients regardless of managers, agents, business managers, and family members. That was the case with Barry. I saw and spoke with him all the time. Barry is gregarious and intensely interested in his career and deals. He also had the great benefit of Garry.

Both are brilliant, but Garry focused on business and Barry on his creative genius. I think Garry may have had a couple of other clients back then in his Stiletto Management business, but the only one he has ever devoted his enormous energy and creative talent to is Barry Manilow.

What an honor to work with him through so many hit records, tours, and TV shows.

✦

I don't know when I realized that Barry and Garry were life partners as well as client and manager. I knew Barry had been married. So had Garry. In fact, Garry had a couple of kids he spoke of all the time. By the time I met him, Barry was newly single and blaming the split on his passion for music and all the time he had to spend away from home. However, his wife had the marriage annulled. Maybe I should have connected certain dots, but I didn't. Barry would later say that he loved her and their divorce wasn't due to sexual orientation.

Barry and Garry's closeness was always obvious. They lived together, yet there was still some doubt of their relationship in my mind; they never showed any personal affection in my presence or in public. Ironically, Barry became the absolute favorite crush among millions of women who were known as "Fanilows." Barry never discussed any of it, but clearly the icon felt the Fanilows needed him to be single and "available."

Coincidentally, Clive also later "came out of the closet" and announced he had always been bisexual.

Could Barry have come out? Maybe it would have mattered and maybe not.

They were clearly in love but couldn't show affection in public, which is extremely sad. Here you had a committed couple in work and in love, but they had to keep their eyes on who was watching. They traveled to some of the most beautiful spots in the world but had to make sure that every moment was spent with just a bit of space between them. There could be no PDA, no hand-holding, and no longing looks across a glass of bubbly after a great show.

Despite the stress of having to worry about photographers and the secret slipping out, they remained a solid couple. It was a tough way to live, but I never saw Barry in a bad mood. He had his public life and his private one. Garry did as well. In the decades we worked together, I cannot recall Garry being difficult, yet it must have been tough to keep their personal relationship secret for four decades. It's actually a tribute to their strong union that they could endure this for so long.

Barry didn't officially come out until 2015, after he quietly married Garry at their fifty-three-acre Palm Springs estate in 2014. News of the marriage leaked, which Barry later called "a blessing and a curse." And he didn't discuss it in detail until 2017 with *People* magazine. Barry said it took so long to come out, even after he married his manager and partner, because he was afraid of disappointing the fans.

No one wanted to wreck the multimillion-dollar-grossing fantasy.

But Barry found out that the fans "were so happy [about his marriage]. The reaction was so beautiful," he told *People*— "strangers commenting, 'Great for you!' I'm just so grateful for it." One fan took to Twitter to write: "Barry Manilow came out!? Who didn't know? Who cares. He's married. Mazel Tov!"

Despite all the success, Barry hasn't changed. Hit after hit and year after year, he is always kind, courteous, and truly a homebody. He is able to do a show on tour and then live a fairly normal life with his partner. At all times, Barry is electric, funny, and truly charming. Garry is as well.

✦

A few years ago, I was at a dinner in Los Angeles for BMI, and there was Garry, walking around, talking to everyone. Meanwhile, Barry sat at a table with his favorite songwriter, Allee Willis. Garry is the extrovert; Barry brings it all to the stage.

Both are still magic.

I love these guys, and they love each other. They are truly an amazing couple.

17

OLIVIA NEWTON-JOHN CONQUERS AMERICA (AND UNIVERSAL)

It was my life, my career, and my music at stake . . .
That was my first nasty experience in the business,
and I decided I'd let John handle it all in the future . . .
The lesson was: you can't go around a problem.
You have to go through it.
—Olivia Newton-John, *Don't Stop Believin'*

Back in 1974, I had been practicing for just three years, but I was at a very good entertainment law firm and had already been in the music business as an artist for twenty years. I went to law school to represent artists after having seen and even signed some unscrupulous contracts from those whom I refer to even now as "exploiters of talent." I was fortunate to learn from some very good mentors and, frankly, from being at the bottom of the totem pole. The good news about that was I got stuck with everything, and I learned by the seat of my pants. Still, the main thing you need to be successful as an entertainment lawyer is clients.

Fortunately, one came into my life that year and stayed with me. We made a wonderful team until she passed away in 2022.

The world mourned along with her friends and family. She was a gift to all, especially to me.

Her name: Olivia Newton-John.

✦

By the time I met Olivia, she was already an international phenomenon, with hits including "If You Love Me (Let Me Know)" and the now iconic "I Honestly Love You." Her manager was Lee Kramer, who also happened to be her fiancé. Lee wanted total control of her career, but he didn't have a law degree and couldn't handle record company deals and contracts. She had an attorney at the time, but Lee didn't like him and she had never met him. Her business manager recommended me, so Lee scheduled a meeting. If it went well, I would meet Olivia.

Meeting number one was just me, Lee, and Olivia's business manager. Olivia was on tour at the time. From the start, I knew that Olivia Newton-John (ONJ) had it all: the angelic voice, the beautiful face, 100 percent heart, and she was a do-gooder who partied with her pups at home. She would do anything for animals. She also crossed genres, weaving between country and pop with the greatest of ease.

ONJ was an original, an Aussie who'd learned her craft in London and came to the United States to conquer the world. Every man wanted to date her, and most young women wanted to be her. She was on the cusp of major stardom when our worlds collided. At the time, she had a great business manager in Joel Jacobson, whose office was close to my firm's. Joel came to that first meeting with Lee and me.

Lee was a guy who wanted answers. He didn't mince words. "Do you want to be Olivia's lawyer?" he asked.

"Yes," I replied. "But first I'd actually like to meet her."

"I can arrange that," Lee said.

Even in my younger days, I never felt comfortable representing someone I hadn't met, so I flew to New York City, where Olivia was performing at the Metropolitan Opera House. The Met was one of the biggest shows of her career, and the pressure was on. "If you go to the show, you can meet her," Joel and Lee said.

I was excited for a couple of reasons. I had never been to the Met, and I wanted to hear Olivia sing live in this legendary setting. I took a good look at her album covers and listened to every record she had ever made. I saw the potential of her becoming an international superstar. So, I got on a plane and flew to New York with no plan in mind, no pitch to deliver. I just hoped Lee remembered to save me a seat and get me the coveted laminated backstage pass. He did, so I just walked up the stage stairs and wandered around until I found Olivia's dressing room.

Dressing rooms are often packed with people: costume designers, makeup artists, PR pros, journalists, etc. It's usually a highly charged atmosphere with bowls of M&Ms and warm sodas. Many artists to this day have pre-stage rituals that they must go through, like prayer or meditation or eating only hummus or Doritos before they walk out there. Silly? Maybe. But until I sing in front of a packed crowd at the Met, I'll reserve judgment.

Olivia had her own thing. When I knocked on the dressing room door, she opened it and then ran for the trash can, where she promptly threw up. Luckily, we were the only two in the room.

"That was kind of weird, wasn't it?" she said to me as I handed her a tissue.

"I'm John," I said. "Are you okay?"

"I'm embarrassed," she said.

The upchucking left no time to talk, so I went to my seat and watched her do an amazing show. The set list was an eclectic mix of her hits to date, including "Please Mr. Please," "Sam," and "Have You Never Been Mellow," combined with soaring covers of "Jolene," "Ring of Fire," "Take Me Home, Country Roads," and "As Time Goes By," and the final showstopper of "I Honestly Love You," which she closed with the rest of her career. If you never had the chance to see Olivia live, then you missed something great. Backstage after the show, after the waves of standing Os, encores, and several curtain calls, she and I met up again. And why not?

She didn't say hello again when I found her backstage and riding the high from a historic performance.

"I hear you're my lawyer," ONJ said as soon as I walked in.

"Yes, if you want me to be."

"Well, I'm going to be in Malibu in three weeks. We'll spend a few hours together there at my house," she said.

Seriously, I'm going to go to Olivia Newton-John's house in Malibu? I thought. *And this is the prerequisite to becoming her lawyer?*

Life was good . . . and getting better by the day.

✦

A few weeks later, I pulled up to the gate at what was an expansive property with a beautiful white house, almost Midwestern in style. Sally Field used to own the place, and I could see why. You could smell the salt from the ocean and feel the sea breeze on your face. ONJ called the place Big Rock, only because that was the name of the street she lived on in Malibu. The "ranch" was also her rock—a place to decompress, relax, and live a bit of a personal life before another tour.

She had a barn filled with horses and a riding arena. The actual house was beautiful with walls of glass windows and vaulted ceilings. She even had an old-fashioned front porch. The estate was a wonderful sanctuary with wild birds and trails where she could ride her horses up into the hills with a pack of her dogs following behind. Anything on four legs was treated like her child, especially her beloved Irish setter named Jackson. Olivia adored animals of all shapes, sizes, and breeds. There were the horses: Judge, a quarter horse (Olivia's favorite); Copy Jay, a Tennessee walker; Eloise, an Appaloosa filly; George; Alex; and Pipes. The dogs included Zargon, Domino, and Gretchen—all Great Danes— plus Jackson. And then there was the cat who always stood up for herself named Gypsy. At the family memorial for Olivia, her husband, John Easterling, brought tears to my eyes when he talked about Olivia's love and respect for all living things.

Some big performers blow their early money on clothes and jewelry. Olivia's biggest expense was her animals, their food, and the people who took care of them when she was touring. When she was home, she did it herself. Always a fan of natural foods, there were huge veggie gardens planted and harvested by Olivia herself to maintain a healthy lifestyle before people had healthy lifestyles.

Lee wasn't around that day, but Olivia's assistant Dana Sharpe held down the fort. One thing about Olivia: She was loyal. Dana was with her from the 1970s until the August when Olivia passed away. Dana, in many ways, ran her social life and kept all the appointments straight, plus so much more. Dana was her rock.

"She's out by the pool," Dana said.

You're meeting Olivia Newton-John by her pool. If nothing else, this will be a good story, I decided.

You couldn't miss her.

Olivia was lying out in a bikini with dark sunglasses on. It was extremely Hollywood. Here we were at a "meeting"—the big music star getting a tan, plus me! Pass the sunscreen. Dana brought us some iced tea, and we caught up on her life and filled in the blanks with background stories.

She didn't like the fact that she never even knew her original lawyers, which was not how she liked to do business. She wanted to know her inner team and wanted involvement in her business affairs, which was smart. There are artists who just want to focus on their art, but that wasn't the case here. Olivia wanted a team around her that she trusted as she called the shots.

We started working together on that day in 1974, after we visited the horses and played with all the dogs. Forty-eight years later, we were still talking or texting at least twice a week. She always answered her own phone and always opened her personal mail.

That was Olivia. She touched lives all over the world with her compassion and life.

✦

From that day on there was nothing about her life that I wasn't involved in. Yes, Lee was doing a good job as her manager, but he needed help with business, including deals for music, tours, videos, merchandise, television, and film. In fact, we even negotiated a movie development deal with Universal Pictures. It was a smart move. We already had a relationship with Universal, which owned her record company, MCA. Lee and Olivia even got offices there on the lot.

But then things hit the skids, as they often do in Hollywood. Lee got heavily into coke and became abusive to everyone on the team, including Olivia, who was always so independent and positive. One day, Lee called a meeting at Universal for him, me, and ONJ. She was in a chair to my right with Lee sitting behind his big desk. He was being his new pompous-ass self.

He looked right at Olivia and said, "You know, I'm in charge, but John has taken control. Either he goes or I go."

She looked up at him. "I guess you're gone," Olivia said.

Lee was furious to the point that he was breathing hard and shouting. "I quit!" he roared.

"Okay," she said in her usual calm voice.

And we both walked out.

"That was incredible," I said after the coast was clear. "I can't believe it."

By the way, their engagement ended eight weeks later, proving business and love in Hollywood can be an awkward affair. Yet, I do want to add here that twenty years later, Lee got sober and fulfilled one of his AA obligations by personally calling me and Olivia to apologize.

✦

Cut to 1977. Olivia was super excited about a new opportunity and called me.

"I've been asked to be in this movie. It's called *Grease*," she said. "Have you heard of the play?"

"I've heard of it," I said, adding, "Olivia, you're twenty-nine, how can you play a teenager in high school?"

"I've thought about that and I'm worried about it, but it's going to be great. John Travolta is in it. It's going to be so big. The whole cast will look the same age."

Incredibly, John Travolta (JT), already cast as Danny, threatened to drop out of the film if ONJ wasn't his Sandy. I still doubt she would have been given the role without his support. He had already starred in the hit television show *Welcome Back, Kotter* and in the massively successful film *Saturday Night Fever*.

It was one of my first lessons in how ONJ had the uncanny ability to pick exactly the right project for herself. Yes, she fretted about the age thing and almost turned the role down. But then JT visited her at her Malibu house and rode horses with her. He even begged her to come to Paramount to do a screen test, which she didn't want to do.

It doesn't usually go like this, but JT himself met her at the gate and escorted her to hair and makeup, where she was instantly transformed into high school girl Sandy. They did their screen test by performing the drive-in scene from the movie where he gets a little too randy in the car, and it was abundantly clear that no one else on earth could play these roles except for John Travolta and Olivia Newton-John. Their chemistry . . . well, it was "electrifying."

Every step of the way, she kept me posted on what was happening. "John Farrar is writing new songs. And Barry Gibb, too," she told me. Those tunes were not in the original play, but it didn't matter. They were amazing cuts and were destined to be hit singles. Farrar wrote and produced all of Olivia's biggest hits, including the number one hit singles "Have You Never Been Mellow," "Magic," and, for the movie, "You're the One That I

Want" and "Hopelessly Devoted to You." He became the coproducer of the *Grease* soundtrack.

As for her deal, I was able to negotiate a sweet one. The Paramount movie contract was solid, but I added a little twist. I called JT's lawyer, and we decided that whatever one got for making *Grease*, the other one got. He agreed, which made the *Grease* contracts phenomenal, including hefty royalties for the use of their faces on the album cover. Everything Sandy and Danny still requires her half of an approval, with JT being the other half.

The plan was for the studio to release the best songs before the movie came out, so the public could sing along to the film. Genius. In rocket speed, those Farrar songs went number one, as did "Grease," written by Barry Gibb and performed by my friend and client Frankie Valli.

"Do you really think I can play seventeen?" Olivia still fretted before cameras rolled.

"This is a different *Grease*," I reminded her. "There was no Australian in the stage play. Think of this as *your* version of *Grease*."

I do have to say that the producer Allan Carr, who first asked her to do the role, was an amazing talent, as was *Grease* director Randal Kleiser. Travolta was the best, as was the rest of the cast, including Didi Conn, who played Frenchy and became a great friend to Olivia for life. Allan and Randal made sure the entire cast was at least twenty-five so all the "high schoolers" looked the same age.

It's always a bonus in this business to surround yourself with a bunch of great people. It's not always that way, but *Grease* stands out as that fantastic, once-in-a-lifetime project when everyone involved represents the very peak of excellence.

I was there on the set the day they shot "You're the One That I Want." Olivia had played what she called "Good Sandy" or "Sandy #1" for most of the shoot. No one in the cast or crew had a clue what Bad Sandy, a.k.a. Sandy #2, would look like. You can imagine the shock when she walked out of her trailer with the teased hair, the red lipstick, the slick top, and those skintight black pants that were sewn onto her. (Later, she would auction the pants off to raise money for her Olivia Newton-John Cancer Wellness and Research Centre in Australia.) The red shoes? They came from her closet. Even the crew guys did double takes, as in, *Who the hell is this? And why haven't we hit on her before?* She was thrilled to hear the whistles and experience the stares, because this movie needed a big ending.

JT was the one who told her the dance number needed a "cap." I stood there watching as she sang and then jumped high and wrapped her legs around his waist as he danced both of them across the high school field. I got to talk to JT at the memorial for Olivia that her family hosted back in September 2022. We discussed that final scene, and he got that big grin he is famous for and said, "It was movie magic."

He and Olivia remained the closest of friends for the rest of her life.

✦

In 1978, Olivia was in a long-term contract with EMI Records, which was known as the Beatles' record company. I hadn't done the original contract with EMI, but I read it carefully and noted that by November of that year, EMI had an option to extend the terms of the contract for three more years. The contract said the label could extend only in writing, rather than the usual automatic extension where no one really talks about it. We didn't have email in those days. *Tick, tick, tick.* The clock kept moving, and I waited until the option date expired.

"Sorry, guys," I wrote to them by mail. "You didn't exercise your option with Olivia, so she is no longer on your label."

No one responded, so after a few weeks went by, I called Bob Mercer, head of EMI.

"EMI didn't formally exercise the option, Bob. What happened?" I asked him.

"We fucked up," he said. "We want to do a new deal with Olivia. Come to London and we will talk about it."

So, I got on a plane, met with Bob Mercer, and made a spectacular deal that included the unheard-of clause that ONJ would own her masters. Her earlier masters had only been licensed to EMI (later, we got those back as well). MCA was licensed as well, but only in North America; EMI was the rest of the world. Olivia stayed at EMI for years.

In 1978, there was also the issue of management. Before Lee "quit," he brought in Roger Davies, who took over shortly thereafter, which was perfect because he had previous experience working as a manager for Tina Turner and Janet Jackson. He ended up having to leave Olivia's camp because Tina needed him more, and later he became Pink's and Sade's manager. I was disappointed that he resigned because he was the right manager at that time.

When Roger left, ONJ's personal appearance agent, Danny Cleary, became her manager. He never gained Olivia's confidence, as truly he had no idea what he was doing, while his partners, Sandy Gallin and Raymond Katz, had extensive experience and success in management and production. Cleary had only been a talent booker. Olivia was very unhappy and called to ask me to let him go. She didn't like controversy or personal confrontations, so I called Joel Jacobson, and we set up a meeting with Danny.

When we were ushered into his office, he looked up and said, "You're here to fire me, aren't you?"

We turned around and walked out. There was nothing more to say.

✦

After the disappointments of Lee Kramer, Danny Cleary, and Roger Davies's resignation, Olivia decided to take a break from managers to manage herself. That left me in the uncomfortable position of responding to everyone on the planet who wanted to do something for or with the superstar.

It was difficult, and I still have incredible respect for honest, hardworking managers. I tried and tried to get Olivia to meet with managers I knew and trusted, and finally, in 1992, she agreed to bring in Mark Hartley. He met all the criteria of honesty, integrity, and experience. They made a great team, and Mark continues, even after ONJ's passing, to advise John Easterling, Olivia's daughter, Chloe, and Primary Wave, which purchased her intellectual property in 2019 when she again became seriously ill.

He is a true partner in every sense.

✦

The late 1970s meant renegotiating Olivia's contract with MCA, which wasn't an easy process. In fact, it turned into a major lawsuit resulting in a famous case that made nationwide headlines. I didn't like the terms MCA proposed for a new contract, so I sent the company a letter saying that Olivia's contract was now terminated for several reasons, including its failure to adequately promote and advertise her music. The *Grease* soundtrack, by the way, came out on RSO Records, not MCA.

The old contract contained these terms: an initial two-year term and three one-year options to follow for a total of five years. It had already been seven years, but MCA argued that the contract could extend past the seven-year mark because Olivia hadn't delivered five albums and insisted that she still owed it additional albums under the old contract. No one could deliver and have success with five albums in five years. MCA sued Olivia, filing an injunction against her signing with any other label.

The powerful and influential Lew Wasserman headed up Universal Pictures, which owned her label. He and his number two, the tenacious Sid Sheinberg, asked for a sit-down with me to talk. I told Olivia that I was going into battle mode, and her reply shocked me.

"Is there any chance I could meet with Mr. Wasserman before we are in litigation?" she asked.

My response? "No way!"

This was not the way you handle disputes. The artist is never in the room, especially for tense meetings. That's what we "talent warriors" do.

"I need to have my own voice," insisted ONJ.

I scheduled the meeting, but there was the inevitable twist. Lew didn't want a face-to-face with Olivia. He said no this time around. The chairman, who had been a talent agent, didn't want to insult the artist if this thing became heated. He didn't want to say things he couldn't take back and have a sour relationship with Olivia. It was better that way, he insisted.

Olivia wouldn't take no for an answer.

I tried again—and shocker, Lew relented and said Olivia could attend.

Lew was going to prove to both of us who was really in charge here. He did have a strong hand, and I knew it!

✦

A few weeks later, Olivia and I were in the elevator at Universal headquarters (then known as "Black Rock"), heading to the top floor to face one of the toughest men in the entertainment business. Lew was savvy, experienced, and knew how to win.

"How are you feeling now?" I asked Olivia.

"Terrified!" she said. "That man scares the hell out of me!"

I had to admire her gutsy move in an age when most women didn't feel they had the power in the music business to make that kind of demand. Hell, most men would sprint away from facing Lew Wasserman in a game of contract chicken.

And we were meeting in his office. Talk about home court advantage.

We waited in the outer room until it was "time," and we were ushered into one of the more unusual offices I've ever been in. Lew had this huge desk that was on some kind of gradual ramp, so it was higher than anything else in the room. He would sit up there—the ultimate ruler of his domain—and stare down at the peons below. The place was designed to make you feel small, while he was Oz.

I felt as if we were having an audience with a king. He sat on his throne, and we sat on dark, formal furniture in this elegant palatial setting, designed to intimidate in every way.

The few pleasantries gave way to business.

Lew gazed down at us through his famously thick glasses and made it clear that he would not let Olivia out of her contract because her records brought in top dollars. He insisted that she owed MCA two additional albums, and he would never let her go or even improve her deal until she delivered them. He was intimidating in every way.

All in all, he said it nicely enough to Olivia. He didn't scream or act angry. There were no threats. There was just his way. He said what he needed to in a matter-of-fact tone that indicated that he wasn't sweating it. He always got his way. Furthermore, Universal's president, Sid Sheinberg, famously always said that he saw "litigation as a profit center for MCA." Kind of funny. I had heard those same words back in 1972 when I was there on behalf of Jack Lemmon.

Olivia walked out of the meeting holding back tears.

I tried to console her, saying what she did was brave, especially since she was never aggressive by nature. It was an illuminating day because I learned again that Olivia doesn't back down. She wouldn't seek trouble, but she wasn't afraid of it.

The tears came from the idea that MCA owned her.

In the end, MCA filed a lawsuit against Olivia for injunctive relief, and we went to court. We lost the first round but pushed on until the California Courts of Appeal changed the verdict and we won.

It was a groundbreaking case for all recording artists. The verdict was that Olivia could leave the label, but MCA could sue for damages, which it did not want to do as it would have had to open its books for our inspection to prove its profits. I would have loved to see the many ways MCA and the other major ex-ploiters of talent made "mistakes" while interpreting contract clauses, always in their favor, amid double-dipping and hiding every ball they hold. So, instead, the label offered a new deal, the one I wanted in the first place, before the war.

From that point on, Olivia owned all her albums and videos for the rest of her career, including the megahit "Physical." Our win also helped countless other artists, who now were able to extricate themselves from exploitative contracts, citing the seven-year precedent set by our case: No forced servitude, even for artists.

✦

Olivia was about so much more than music, but one question remained. How could she follow up a hit like *Grease*, the film that made her a huge movie star and that to date has earned a shade under $400 million worldwide? (Not bad when you consider that the film was made for $6 million back in 1978.) Both JT and Olivia nixed *Grease 2* because the script wasn't as good as the original.

By 1979, she was filming *Xanadu*, which included singing, dancing, and even roller-skating. Her dance number with Gene Kelly—filmed in a room with just the director, a cameraman, and the two of them—was a career highlight.

There was other magic on that set. While shooting, Olivia met a young dancer named Matthew Lattanzi, and the two fell in love. They married, and Olivia went through a blissful time of nesting during her pregnancy with her beloved daughter, Chloe. The marriage lasted ten years, and we quietly negotiated the divorce at her kitchen table. Even when things didn't work out the way Olivia planned, they still worked it out for their daughter.

Olivia, whose world shattered when her parents divorced, refused to be involved in some drawn-out, public spectacle. Olivia, Matt, and I, along with a judge serving as the mediator, sat in her home figuring out how to make this as easy as possible for their daughter. Olivia wanted her daughter to have a healthy relationship with her father. The final decree mandated that Olivia was the primary caretaker, but Matt would live close by and Chloe could see him anytime she wanted.

Olivia and Matt remained friends until the end, with Chloe being their most important link. Olivia's second husband, John Easterling, also fostered a wonderful relationship with Chloe throughout their marriage and even invited Matt to Olivia's personal memorial, where Matt joined hands with Chloe and spoke fondly of those happier days and their love of their daughter.

It was just love, the way Olivia would have wanted it. And you had to believe that was magic.

✦

"John, I simply cannot do it," Olivia said when the song "Physical" (written by Terry Shaddick and her longtime friend Steve Kipner) came her way. "I can't sing the lyrics 'Let me hear your body talk.' Please!"

Roger Davies was sure it would be a hit and would pave the way for a whole new image. Olivia still thought the lyrics were a bit too sexy. True fact: Tina Turner was given the song first and turned it down for that reason. It was Tina who suggested to Roger that they offer it to Olivia, because, really, who would expect ONJ to sing those words?

"I love it. It's a total image changer," I said.

"They want me to sing 'You gotta know that you're bringin' out the animal in me,'" she countered.

"Edgy," I said.

"John, the lyrics have me singing 'There's nothin' left to talk about unless it's horizontally'! I'm worried the fans won't embrace it," she said.

In the end, Roger calmed her fears. "She was concerned that she would lose her wholesome girl-next-door image. I told her, 'Don't worry, you can blame me.'"

The song was a phenomenal hit and spent ten weeks on top of the Billboard Hot 100. When radio stations banned the racy song, we sold even more copies. The video was a worldwide sensation and earned her a Grammy. This led to 1982's North America Physical Tour and a flood of publicity. It marked the height of her solo career and made her one of the most successful female artists of the early 1980s. She loved it!

Her choppy haircut also swept the nation. Leotards were the fashion at all the gyms in the world. She changed her look dramatically. On the other hand, after both the phenomenal hits of *Grease* and "Physical," Olivia remained exactly the same person as when I met her at the Met.

✦

In 1992, Olivia told me that she had breast cancer and would have a partial mastectomy followed by chemotherapy and breast reconstruction. Bianca and I were devastated and, as a tribute, named one of our daughters who was born later that year Olivia. We always called our daughter "Little Olivia," especially to "Big Olivia."

As with all adversity I watched her face, Olivia not only took this diagnosis calmly but decided to use it as an opportunity to promote wellness. She had her treatments and the cancer went into remission, but it returned in 2013 as a tumor in her shoulder that became a cancer at the base of her spine. This time she had an inoperable tumor, but she still continued to perform and carry on her philanthropic efforts with grace and a smile. I never heard Olivia complain. She always used her experiences and knowledge to help others in need. And she never said, *Why me?* She only said, "Why not me? Maybe my purpose in life is to help others get through health issues like mine."

ONJ helped raise funds in 2008 to build the Olivia Newton-John Cancer Research and Wellness Centre in Melbourne, Australia, which provides expert care for patients while also conducting groundbreaking cancer research including global research into plant medicine. She stayed and was cared for there in 2021. Olivia would joke that her stay was an episode of *Undercover Boss*. She also made sure to always wear a little hat to disguise herself, and not because she craved privacy. She didn't want to take away any attention from the other patients.

✦

Olivia and I would spend decades together, and she will forever be one of my most important and beloved clients. She not only knew my birthday but Bianca's and each of our kids', sending presents every year. At Christmas, we received not only a gift but a wonderful handwritten note. We had a special bond and a shorthand that was similar to one between a brother and a sister. We had one of those things where we communicated with just a glance. "Just handle it, John," she would say. If she said it once, she said it a million times.

Something magical happened to Olivia at age fifty-nine. She found the love of her life in John Easterling. They first met in the early 1990s and later bonded since they both had dogs from the same litter. For their first date, she joined him in the Amazon, where he had a home to study natural medicine. They married in 2008, a year after they began dating. Their wedding was a spiritual ceremony in Peru and then a legal wedding in Florida. They were an amazing couple who remained deeply in love.

Olivia died on August 8, 2022.

After she passed, John wrote these words to her: "Olivia, our love for each other transcends our understanding. Every day, we expressed our gratitude for this love that could be so deep, so real and so natural. We accepted the experience of our love as past, present and forever."

She was so lucky to find John, who is a stand-up guy and super smart. He helped to give her a life she loved at their ranch outside of Santa Barbara with their horses and dogs. He worked hard using herbs and natural ways to alleviate her pain and promote healing, buying her extra years via plant treatments. I don't think she would have survived so long without his help. John and Chloe hosted a magical celebration of her life with friends and family on September 21, 2022. It was moving, and we all felt her presence.

Three months before Olivia passed, she invited Bianca and me to visit her. When we arrived, she needed assistance to move but still gave us the hug and smile we had known for decades. We made our way out to the back, and within minutes, she was cracking jokes and exercising her wit.

She was optimistic about recovery and said John agreed to take her to Florida if she gained five pounds. She was excited to have adopted a service dog, which was already in training and would arrive at their house in September. ONJ laughed and said, "You will never guess his name—Jackson." It was the name of her beloved first dog whom I had met at her house all the way back in May 1974, forty-eight years earlier.

I imagine Olivia on her horse with Jackson running at her side.

ACKNOWLEDGEMENTS

I had a lot of help along the way. In the stories I have told in this book, I have mentioned many by name. The lawyer back in 1972 who introduced me to music law and a couple of my clients was Seymour Bricken. I might never have learned and succeeded so early without his guidance.

Barry Krost, Tony Scotti, Mike Curb, Conway Twitty, and Jimmy Bowen helped me enormously along the way.

While I wrote a chapter about Olivia Newton-John, I will never be able to give her enough praise. The experience over forty-eight years together was "magic."

This book would never have been written without the urging and enthusiasm of my friend Dr. Paul Kudelko. He is the one person who would just never give up, saying, "John, you gotta write a book." My late-night tequila tastings with him gave me the courage and inspiration for *Crazy Lucky*.

I met my cowriter, Cindy Pearlman Gaber, when Olivia decided to hire her to ghostwrite her book *Don't Stop Believin'*. Cindy spent countless hours with Olivia, listening to her stories. It was Olivia who told me how comfortable Cindy made her feel. Cindy also spent countless hours with me, listening to my seemingly endless stories and capturing them on paper. I would have had no idea how to start or finish this work without her.

I was at a loss about how to publish this book and get it out in the universe where people could find and maybe read it. All the books I had been involved with as a lawyer were by celebrities with the deal set by an agent before there was a book. I also had the honor and fun of representing Jackie Collins, who could have worked with any publisher in the world given her literary success. I was neither a celebrity nor a writer. One day, when asked by my good friend Spencer Proffer what I was working on, I told him the concept for *Crazy Lucky*. He said, "Let me handle it for you." And he has done just that for me. Thank you, Spencer.

One hugely important part of this process is having a great editor with the patience to read the work in process and advise. John Cerullo had the experience and wisdom to make it better. Thank you, John.

When I started this book, I had seven children. We lost our wonderful Loni in 2022. All of them lived some of this story with me, and some were there for almost all of it. Lindsay, Loni, Morgan, Milana, Olivia, Sam, and Julia have given me most of the best times of my life. I hope they, and many generations to come, enjoy the stories and remember their dad and the ancestors who wrote them.

Finally, I acknowledge, thank, and love my wife, Bianca, who made my life complete, encouraged me to keep writing, especially when I quit, lost interest, and abandoned the whole thing. She has made my life a dream come true. I was crazy lucky to meet her and to have spent most of our lives together.

ABOUT THE AUTHOR

Named "Entertainment Lawyer of the Year" by *Billboard Magazine*, **JOHN MASON** has represented a variety of icons in the entertainment industry throughout his career, including notable names in film, television and music and top talent in literary and music publishing, sports and electronic media. He has served as the chairman of the Nevada Film Commission and as a member of the President's Committee on The Arts and Humanities. Mason and his legal work have been highlighted by a variety of prominent publications, including *The Los Angeles Times, The American Lawyer, Los Angeles Magazine, The Wall Street Journal, The Hollywood Reporter, Los Angeles Daily Business Journal, Variety, The New York Times, Reno Gazette Journal,* and *Las Vegas Review.*